MW01259693

THE WORLDS OF

WES
ANDERSON

Quarto

First published in 2024 by Frances Lincoln,
an imprint of The Quarto Group.
One Triptych Place, London, SE1 9SH,
United Kingdom
T (0)20 7700 9000
www.Quarto.com

Text copyright © 2024 Adam Woodward
Design copyright © 2024 Quarto Publishing Plc
Illustrations by Lorena Spurio

Adam Woodward has asserted his moral right
to be identified as the Author of this Work in
accordance with the Copyright Designs and
Patents Act 1988.

All rights reserved. No part of this book may
be reproduced or utilised in any form or by
any means, electronic or mechanical, including
photocopying, recording or by any information
storage and retrieval system, without permission
in writing from Frances Lincoln.

Every effort has been made to trace the
copyright holders of material quoted in this book.
If application is made in writing to the publisher,
any omissions will be included in future editions.

A catalogue record for this book is available
from the British Library.

ISBN 978-0-7112-8216-2
Ebook ISBN 978-0-7112-8217-9

10 9 8 7 6 5 4 3 2 1

Design by Claire Warner

Publisher: Philip Cooper
Senior Commissioning Editor: John Parton
Senior Editor: Laura Bulbeck
Deputy Art Director: Isabel Eeles
Senior Production Controller: Eliza Walsh

Printed in Malaysia

MIX
Paper | Supporting
responsible forestry
FSC® C007207

Disclaimer: This publication and its contents are not licensed,
authorised or connected with Wes Anderson or his work.

Adam
Woodward

THE WORLDS OF

WES
ANDERSON

The Influences and Inspiration
Behind the Iconic Films

FRANCES
LINCOLN

CONTENTS

Introduction
06

INTRODUCTION

I was a card-carrying member of Team Wes long before I started writing about film professionally. The first time I saw *The Royal Tenenbaums* (2001) was in the spring of 2002 during its UK theatrical run at my local cinema, and I later rented *Rushmore* (1998) on DVD from the little video store down the road, where I worked over two consecutive summers. For the past 15 years, I've been on staff at *Little White Lies* magazine, which, incidentally, featured *The Life Aquatic with Steve Zissou* (2004) on its very first cover. During this time, my love for Anderson's work has only grown. I've been fortunate enough to attend world premieres of several of his films, interview some of his closest collaborators and host repertory screenings, lectures and even pub quizzes on all things Wes.

'How well do you know Wes Anderson?' I've been asked this question on numerous occasions over the years, and it was the first question I asked myself when I started this project. Even after the fact, I feel like I've barely scratched the surface of understanding exactly what makes Anderson tick. Indeed, in the early stages of my research, I quickly came to the realization that his influences are remarkably diverse both in origin and in how they manifest themselves. Any attempt to squeeze them all into a single book would not only be impractical but would probably make for a rather uninteresting read.

Therefore, this is not intended to be a definitive or exhaustive guide to the myriad references contained within Anderson's filmography. Think of it as a leisurely treasure hunt – a zigzagging, career-spanning journey into the director's creative process that seeks to uncover and contextualize his most salient inspirations and passions. *The Worlds of Wes Anderson* comprises nine loosely themed chapters, each subdivided into four mini essays, which encompass different narrative and technical aspects of Anderson's filmmaking style. Topics range from absent parents and dead pets to messy break-ups and daring jailbreaks, as well as his bold use of colour, costume and formal techniques, such as one-point perspective (the secret to his perfectly symmetrical compositions).

Such is the strength of Anderson's aesthetic, it is easy to overlook just how intelligent and sophisticated a storyteller he is. Yes, he makes meticulous, moreish confections filled with eccentric characters and outlandish scenarios, but everything he does is rooted in emotional truth – the sugary sweetness and whimsical tone balanced by the same desires, hopes and fears that govern all our lives. The fundamental reason why Anderson's films have gained critical and commercial success and won him fans across the globe is that they reveal something essential about the human experience. They are as relatable as they are delectable.

Whenever I watch one of Anderson's films, I feel an instant connection to the past – to the great filmmakers who came before Anderson whose work has fed his imagination. Crucially, Anderson never pays homage to others simply to prove his cinephilic chops, as many other contemporary directors do. Instead, the references he carefully and confidently threads into the fabric of his films – whether in the form of clothing, music, camera shots or editing tricks – are always in service of the story. And they often reveal something about Anderson himself.

If there's one thing I know about Anderson, it's that he is a truly international filmmaker. Born and raised in Houston, Texas, the son of an archaeologist and a real estate agent, he was exposed to foreign cinema and world literature at a young age. Since filming his first two features, *Bottle Rocket* (1996) and *Rushmore*, in his home state, he has shot films in England, France, Germany, India, Italy, Spain and twice along America's Atlantic Coast. Now approaching his fourth decade as a filmmaker, he continues to draw inspiration from the books he reads, the films he watches, the people he meets and the places he visits, always on the lookout for new adventures and never losing his childlike sense of wonder.

Of course, Anderson's cultural anchors run much deeper than just the film world. So, alongside old masters such as Stanley Kubrick, Jean-Luc Godard and Akira Kurosawa, in these pages you will also find architects, fashion designers, musicians, novelists, painters, poets and photographers – exceptionally talented trailblazers who have all helped shape Anderson's artistic sensibility. Evocations of place and time are also integral to Anderson's work, from pre-war Europe in *The Grand Budapest Hotel* (2014) to mid-century Paris in *The French Dispatch* (2021) to 1960s New England in *Moonrise Kingdom* (2012), while cultural icons such as Jacques-Yves Cousteau, Roald Dahl and the *New Yorker* magazine are obvious touchstones.

For the most part, I have followed a rough course plotted by Anderson himself. In audio commentaries and media interviews, he is often quite candid about where his ideas come from without necessarily going into much detail. At this point, I must acknowledge that I am by no means the first person to excavate Anderson's various sources of inspiration, although I have tried as much as possible to offer my own analysis and insights into the creative choices he makes. The aim of this book is to illustrate and explain why Anderson's films look and feel the way they do, but it also contains personal meditations on some of his lesser-surveyed stylistic and thematic preoccupations.

You may already be familiar with Wes Anderson, or maybe you are a relative newcomer to his world (in which case, welcome to your new obsession). Whatever your relationship to Anderson's films, there is always something new to discover. That is the real joy of watching them. I hope that reading this book leaves you with a deeper appreciation of Anderson's immaculate craft. Perhaps it might even inspire you to broaden your cinematic and cultural horizons. Because, although Anderson is famed for having one of the most reliably consistent and easily identifiable styles of any filmmaker working today, his natural curiosity means he never stops exploring.

BELOW: Lobby boys: Wes Anderson and Jude Law having a discussion on the set of *The Grand Budapest Hotel*.

CHAPTER 1

YOUTH IN REVOLT

'AFTER THIS, I CAN'T LIVE WITH MY PARENTS ANYMORE. I'VE GOT TO DISAPPEAR.' – ANTOINE DOINEL

OPPOSITE: Seeing double: Antoine and René enquire after a classmate's 'fancy glasses', which resemble aviation goggles (top). Dignan sports a similar pair of protective eyewear in *Bottle Rocket* (bottom).

PART 1
Les quatre cents coups

(*The 400 Blows*, François Truffaut, 1959)

In 2014, during an on-stage Q&A at the New York Public Library, Wes Anderson recalled a cinematic epiphany that changed his life. 'I discovered [François] Truffaut in the little video rental section at the back of a record store in Houston when I was 16. [*Les quatre cents coups (The 400 Blows)*] was one of the reasons I started thinking I would like to make movies.' Anderson later told the author and critic Matt Zoller Seitz that *Les quatre cents coups* 'made a huge, rock band-type impression on me.' For a teenage Anderson, watching Truffaut's film was comparable to listening to the Velvet Underground's first record in 1967, where legend has it that everyone who bought a copy started a band of their own.

Les quatre cents coups not only introduced the then 27-year-old Truffaut to the world stage but also kick-started the film movement known as *La Nouvelle Vague*, or French New Wave, which has had a significant and lasting impact on Anderson's filmmaking style. This influence is particularly evident in his proof-of-concept short film *Bottle Rocket* from 1994, with its black-and-white cinematography, handheld *cinéma vérité* (literally 'truthful cinema'; a style of filmmaking that seeks to provide an authentic and unfiltered portrayal of people and events) camerawork and light jazz soundtrack. There are traces of Truffaut and *La Nouvelle Vague* in Anderson's early features, too.

In both versions of *Bottle Rocket* (1994 and 1996), Anthony (Luke Wilson) and Dignan (Owen Wilson) are shown discussing their latest scheme at a pinball machine,

mirroring the shot in *Les quatre cents coups* of 13-year-old Antoine (Jean-Pierre Léaud) and his best friend René (Patrick Auffay) killing time in a café during their day of truancy. Pinball was a popular pastime of *La Nouvelle Vague*, also featuring in Jean-Luc Godard's 1962 film *Vivre sa vie* (*It's My Life*). Later, when Dignan is arrested following a botched robbery, Anderson evokes the moment when another of Antoine's errant peers is escorted back to the youth detention centre from which he escaped a few days earlier. The iconic image of Antoine's face pressed against a chain-link fence is also alluded to in *Bottle Rocket*'s penultimate shot.

In *Rushmore* (1998), Max Fischer's (Jason Schwartzman) classroom closely resembles the one in Truffaut's film, where we are first introduced to Antoine. Elsewhere, Max's karting goggles are similar to the 'fancy glasses' worn by one of Antoine's classmates; additionally, this is a reference to a portrait by the French photographer Jacques Henri Lartigue, whom you can read more about in Chapter 9. In both *Les quatre cents coups* and *Rushmore*, a typewriter proves instrumental in determining the fates of our young protagonists: Antoine's theft of his father's Royal office typewriter results in him being sent to the aforementioned reform school; Max uses a portable Brother De Luxe to write the plays through which he processes his grief, the case poignantly inscribed with the words, 'Bravo, Max! Love, Mom'.

After completing his 1957 short film *Les mistons (The Mischief Makers)*, Truffaut envisaged his next project as a 20-minute sketch titled *Antoine Runs Away*. With the help of television writer Marcel Moussy, he eventually fleshed out the idea into a feature-length chronicle of adolescent angst. Based on Truffaut's own experience of growing up in Paris in the 1940s (Antoine was not only semi-autobiographical but something of a cinematic alter ego, appearing in four subsequent films by the director over the next two decades), *Les quatre cents coups* is an unsentimental yet life-affirming look at the awkward intersection between childhood and young adulthood. In many ways Antoine is a typical early teen. He pulls pranks, plays hooky and generally misbehaves. He is naive, rash, rebellious. He also yearns for freedom – from his inattentive parents, authoritarian teachers and, most pointedly, his own painful coming-of-age.

Antoine is above all portrayed as an outsider, a trait that likely endeared him to Anderson. Both *Bottle Rocket* and *Rushmore* centre on insecure yet strong-willed characters who constantly go against the grain of their respective social milieus. Like Antoine before them, Anthony, Dignan and Max are all depicted as impish and imprudent. Crucially, though, we are always on their side because Anderson aligns us with their individual perspectives, just as Truffaut does with Antoine. We are encouraged to empathize with them even when they act in a selfish or underhand way. How do both directors achieve this? The answer lies in how they observe their characters.

Compare the lateral tracking shot at the end of *Les quatre cents coups* with those found in Anderson's films. The fluid motion of Truffaut's camera is motivated not just by the physical movement of the character but by his present mental state. Having fled the youth detention centre, Antoine is shown dashing through the Normandy countryside in a final, desperate bid for freedom. This type of shot has become an Anderson staple, cropping up not only in *Bottle Rocket* and *Rushmore* but across his entire filmography (this is covered in more detail in Chapter 7), often in slow motion for added dramatic impact. It's just one example of how Anderson's singular style is underpinned by both his technical proficiency and his fluency in the language of cinema.

Indeed, perhaps the single most important thing that Anderson acquired from Truffaut is a deeper understanding of the visual grammar of filmmaking, including how the composition, framing and sequencing of images can be utilized to create atmosphere, convey information or elicit a particular emotional response from an audience. Despite the fact that Truffaut was an innovator and risk-taker who challenged French cinema's status quo by experimenting with different formal techniques, he knew the rulebook as well as anyone; he and his *Nouvelle Vague* contemporaries didn't rip it up so much as reimagine it in their own style. Anderson may not be as consciously radical as Truffaut, but his work still has all the hallmarks of a highly inventive, staunchly independent artist.

OPPOSITE: Anderson repurposes the chain link fence shot from *Les quatre cents coups* (second from top) in both *Bottle Rocket* (top) and *Rushmore* (third from top).

Dignan's arrest (bottom left) evokes the recapture of one of Antoine's fellow juvies (bottom right).

LEFT: The official French theatrical poster for *Les quatre cents coups*.

ABOVE: Both *Rushmore* (top) and *Les quatre cents coups* (bottom) open with scenes set in the classrooms of their respective protagonists.

OPPOSITE: The American photographer Robert Mapplethorpe in 1979 (left), who was the inspiration for Robert Musgrave's character in *Bottle Rocket* (right).

WHAT ABOUT BOB?

Robert Musgrave, a longtime associate of Anderson and the Wilson brothers, appears in both versions of *Bottle Rocket* as the getaway driver and reluctant third wheel in Anthony and Dignan's dysfunctional gang. Musgrave's character is referred to throughout simply as 'Bob'. But in the feature-length *Bottle Rocket*, he is credited as Bob Mapplethorpe in reference to the groundbreaking and somewhat controversial New York photographer Robert Mapplethorpe, who gained a reputation for his striking, often homoerotic black-and-white portraits, nudes and still lives before tragically dying of AIDS in 1989.

Anderson has made it a tradition to pay tribute to famous people in this way. Think of Dr Nelson Guggenheim in *Rushmore*, named after the prominent art collector and socialite Peggy Guggenheim, or Dudley Heinsbergen in *The Royal Tenenbaums* (2001), after the muralist and interior designer Anthony Heinsbergen, or the Whitman brothers in *The Darjeeling Limited* (2007), after the humanist poet and essayist Walt Whitman, or Edward Norton's Conrad Earp in *Asteroid City* (2023), after the novelist Joseph Conrad and the legendary frontiersman Wyatt Earp. While Anderson is a known admirer of Mapplethorpe's work, however, it's likely that he gave Musgrave's character this moniker as an in-joke between old friends.

'YOU KNOW THIS CITY'S FULL OF HAWKS?
THAT'S A FACT.' – TERRY MALLOY

OPPOSITE: Wiretap: Terry attempts to woo Edie from behind chicken wire, appearing caged like the pigeons he has taken a fancy to (top). In *The Royal Tenenbaums*, when Royal first meets his grandsons Ari and Uzi on the roof of the 375th Street Y, he is framed in a similar fashion (bottom).

PART 2
On the Waterfront

(Elia Kazan, 1954)

In the mid-1950s, American cinema underwent a profound transformation as audiences started demanding more complex and relatable characters, as well as greater narrative realism. Freed from the shackles of the old studio system, a new generation of filmmakers emerged armed with politically charged, socially conscious dramas such as *The Man with the Golden Arm* (1955), *The Night of the Hunter* (1955) and *12 Angry Men* (1957). One of the chief architects of this paradigm shift was Elia Kazan, a Turkish-born *émigré* who collaborated with playwrights Arthur Miller and Tennessee Williams on Broadway before breaking boundaries in Hollywood with *A Streetcar Named Desire* (1951), *On the Waterfront* and *East of Eden* (1955) – all studio pictures that reflected a changing social mood and an industry in flux.

On the Waterfront, a story of racketeering and romance on the Jersey shore, is told from the perspective of Marlon Brando's granite-tough anti-hero, Terry Malloy, an ex-prize fighter who doesn't know when he's beaten. Set in the hardscrabble docklands of Hoboken, the film depicts a blue-collar community that is being exploited by a crooked union boss, ironically named Johnny Friendly (Lee J. Cobb). The directionless Terry, who we later learn has been kept down his whole life by his connected older brother Charley (Rod Steiger), is caught in the middle. But he sees a way out when he meets a young woman from the neighbourhood named Edie (Eva Marie Saint), who is investigating the suspicious death of her brother Joey.

Aside from Brando's famous 'I coulda been a contender' monologue, the most renowned moment in *On the Waterfront* – and the one that typifies Kazan's boundary-pushing filmmaking style – occurs when Terry confesses to Edie that he had a role in Joey's murder. Standing on a pile of rubble overlooking the Hudson River, with the Manhattan skyline obscured by smog from the nearby shipyard, the one-time pugilist spills his guts. But we barely catch a word of it. Kazan muffles Terry's admission with the sound of passing steamboats and heavy machinery, the expression on Edie's face as she learns the awful truth telling us everything we need to know.

As noted by Matt Zoller Seitz in *The Wes Anderson Collection* (2013), Anderson emulates this scene in *Rushmore* when Max meets Mrs Blume (played by Kim Terry, who could easily pass for an older and wearier Edie) on top of a multistorey car park to break the news of her husband's infidelity. Max's choice of venue is a poor one. The frigid air and noisy streets below only add to the awkwardness of the occasion; as does the fact that he tries to mitigate his spiteful meddling by serving a conciliatory spread of tuna fish and peanut butter and jelly sandwiches. The scene is accompanied by Donovan's autumn ballad 'Jersey Thursday', which could be an oblique nod to the near-namesake American state of New Jersey where *On the Waterfront* is set.

The stakes may be considerably lower in Anderson's film – although its lovelorn protagonist might beg to differ – but this example shows that, when done right, homage can be a useful tool for communicating a feeling or mood to an audience. It's worth noting that *Rushmore* and *On the Waterfront* also share a casting connection: Seymour Cassel, who plays Max's father, starred in Kazan's 1976 film *The Last Tycoon*, which coincidentally gave another Anderson regular, Anjelica Huston, one of her earliest screen roles.

Anderson's next film, *The Royal Tenenbaums* (2001), contains further allusions to *On the Waterfront*. In Kazan's film, after Joey is killed, Terry is wracked with guilt over his small but decisive role in the crime. To ease his conscience, he decides to take care of Joey's orphaned pigeons, which occupy a large coop on the roof of his apartment building. It is here that Edie first sees a gentler side of Terry, whose flinty exterior masks an inner vulnerability. He introduces her to one of the birds and she softens towards him, ultimately accepting his rather clumsy invitation to take her out for a drink.

The way this exchange is filmed, with each actor framed in close-up, looking at each other through the chicken wire, is matched by Anderson in the scene where Royal Tenenbaum (Gene Hackman) meets his grandsons Ari (Grant Rosenmeyer) and Uzi (Jonah Meyerson) for the first time, along with their pet beagle, Buckley. Although the context is different, both Terry and Royal are equally sincere in trying to strike up a relationship with those on the other side of the fence. It's also telling that Royal is present when Richie (Luke Wilson) and

his trained falcon Mordecai are reunited on the roof of the Lindbergh Palace Hotel.

Birds of prey play their part in *On the Waterfront*, too. Early on in the film, Terry tells Edie that the city is full of hawks that 'hang around on the top of the big hotels'. Without his protection, he explains, the hawks will swoop down and snatch Joey's pigeons – the wider implication being that those who enjoy elevated positions of power always prey on the innocent and weak. In Terry's world, you're either a pigeon or a hawk. The question is whether he will stand with the downtrodden dockers and, by extension, Edie, or the corrupt union bosses to whom he is indebted.

In the end, Terry's conscience wins out. He rejects his avian credo and uses his own hawkish instincts, sharpened by years of brawling in the ring and on the streets, to depose Johnny Friendly by testifying against him and his gang in court. The film's violent finale places us firmly in Terry's corner; his defiance inspires the workers to stand up for themselves and they return to the waterfront emboldened. Although there is a lingering sense that this victory may be temporary – that corruption is likely to return – the moral of *On the Waterfront* is much less ambiguous. *Rushmore* and *The Royal Tenenbaums* end on a similar note, with both Max and Royal realizing that to make amends they must first swallow their pride and exercise a little selflessness.

OPPOSITE: The official US quad poster for *On the Waterfront* (top).

Anderson has said that Elia Kazan (bottom left) was the inspiration for Adrien Brody's character in *Asteroid City* (bottom right). In 1947, Kazan founded the Actors Studio in New York City, another key inspiration for Anderson's film.

WINNER OF 8 ACADEMY AWARDS

BEST PICTURE
Best Actor
Best Supporting Actress
Best Director
Best Story and Screenplay
Best Cinematography
Best Film Editing
Best Art Direction

PACKED WITH POWER AND STRENGTH!

COLUMBIA PICTURES presents

MARLON BRANDO

AN ELIA KAZAN PRODUCTION

ON THE WATERFRONT

co-starring
KARL MALDEN · LEE J. COBB · with Rod Steiger · Pat Henning · and EVA MARIE SAINT
Produced by SAM SPIEGEL · Screen Play by BUDD SCHULBERG · Music by LEONARD BERNSTEIN · Directed by ELIA KAZAN

WHEN DONE RIGHT, HOMAGE CAN BE A USEFUL TOOL FOR COMMUNICATING A FEELING OR MOOD TO AN AUDIENCE

OPPOSITE: Love theme: Marlon Brando and Eva Marie Saint's chemistry is palpable in this official publicity still (top). Margot and Richie share a smoke while reconciling on the roof of the Tenenbaum mansion (bottom).

ABOVE: Terry's heart-wrenching confession to Edie (left) is riffed on by Anderson in *Rushmore* when Max sabotages his romantic rival's marriage (right).

IN TERRY'S WORLD,
YOU'RE EITHER A
PIGEON OR A HAWK

'ANARCHY IS THE ONLY SLIGHT GLIMMER OF HOPE.'
– MICK JAGGER

OPPOSITE: Needle drop: The Rolling Stones posing in Green Park, London in 1967 (top). In *The Royal Tenenbaums*, Margot drops the needle on a US mono pressing of the Stones' fifth studio album *Between the Buttons* (bottom), from 1967.

PART 3
The British Invasion

(1964–67)

The concept of a jukebox soundtrack, where pre-existing popular music is used to complement or juxtapose the action in a scene, was pioneered by two American films from 1973: George Lucas's *American Graffiti* and Martin Scorsese's *Mean Streets*, the latter of which had a formative impact on Anderson, as discussed in Chapter 8. Anderson has followed in this tradition by employing an eclectic mix of musical cues throughout his career, including 'Needle in the Hay' by Elliott Smith (released 1995, used in *The Royal Tenenbaums*), '30 Century Man' by Scott Walker (released 1969, used in *The Life Aquatic with Steve Zissou*, 2004), 'Les Champs-Élysées' by Joe Dassin and 'Le temps de l'amour' by Françoise Hardy (released 1969 and 1962 respectively, used in *Moonrise Kingdom*, 2012), among others. But it's the enduring countercultural sound of the British Invasion, particularly the Kinks and the Rolling Stones, that Anderson is most attuned to.

This further marks Anderson as a Scorsese disciple: *Mean Streets* features the Rolling Stones' 'Jumpin' Jack Flash' (1968) and 'Tell Me' (1964) on its soundtrack, the beginning of a decades-long love affair between director and band that culminated in the 2008 Scorsese-helmed concert film *Shine a Light*. To date, Anderson has used no fewer than six of their songs in his films. (As a side note, *The Darjeeling Limited*, 2007, was the first to feature the Rolling Stones on its official soundtrack. *Bottle Rocket*, *Rushmore* and *The Royal Tenenbaums* each contain songs by the group, but, for contractual reasons, they do not appear on the corresponding soundtrack albums.) So, what does Anderson's preoccupation with the Rolling Stones, and British 1960s rock music in general, reveal about his work?

In *Bottle Rocket*, during the break-in at Hinckley Cold Storage, Dignan declares 'they'll never catch me, man, 'cause I'm fuckin' innocent!' before running back inside to rescue one of his accomplices. As this is happening, the song '2000 Man', taken from the Rolling Stones' 1967 LP *Their Satanic Majesties Request*, fades up. The song's philosophical lyrics describe an anonymous man of the future whose name is just a number, alienated from his kids and hooked on modern technology. It portrays the kind of dreary existence that Dignan has firmly rejected by casting himself as an intrepid outlaw who's not afraid to dream big. Scorsese himself praised Anderson's use of the song in a 2000 *Esquire* editorial, noting that '[Dignan] – and the music – are proclaiming who he really is: he's not innocent in the eyes of the law, but he's truly an innocent. For me, it's a transcendent moment.'

The theme of nonconformity is also prevalent in 'Street Fighting Man', a single from the Rolling Stones' next album, *Beggars Banquet* (1968). Mick Jagger wrote the song in response to the anti-Vietnam War demonstration in London on 17 March 1968, and the student riots and resulting civil unrest that swept through Paris two months later. Anderson, revealing himself as a social history buff as well as a Rolling Stones superfan, uses the song in *Fantastic Mr. Fox* (2009) during 'The Terrible Tractors' sequence in which Mr Fox and co. are forced to dig deep to avoid being crushed by their capitalist oppressors. Later in the film, Mr Fox salutes the mysterious black wolf in a show of solidarity (this is also a reference to Sydney Pollack's 1972 film *Jeremiah Johnson*).

On a less political note, the plaintive 'I Am Waiting' from the 1966 album *Aftermath* is used in *Rushmore* to simultaneously signal the start of November and Max's slide into depression. Anderson told the *A.V. Club* in a 1999 interview:

> With *Rushmore*, I originally had songs I said I wanted to use in the movie, and then I did research in this certain area of music [the British Invasion]. I would just listen to songs and I'd know what should go in there. There's a song by the Stones called 'I Am Waiting,' which I was listening to a lot when I was driving around . . . That whole part of the story evolved out of the feeling that that song has.

Rushmore is also where Anderson first displayed his soft spot for the Kinks. In the typewritten, hand-annotated liner notes to the film's soundtrack, Anderson explains that he originally planned to use only Kinks songs:

> I thought this made sense because the Kinks played loud, angry, teenage rock songs, and they wore blazers and ties; and our movie is about a teenager who is loud and angry, and he is almost never seen without his blazer and tie . . . I eventually expanded this concept to include the whole British Invasion, because they all basically dressed like that.

In the end, only one Kinks song made it into the film: 'Nothin' in the World Can Stop Me Worryin' 'Bout That Girl' from the group's second album, *Kinda Kinks*, released in 1965 (the band's music would feature more heavily in *The Darjeeling Limited*). As Ray Davies sings about being tormented by the thought of losing the woman he is in love with, Herman Blume (Bill Murray) idly tosses golf balls into a swimming pool before slowly ascending to the top of a diving board, downing his whisky soda, and performing the most joyless cannonball in cinematic history.

Among Anderson's other noteworthy needle drops from this era are 'Making Time' by the Creation (1967) in *Rushmore*, right after Brian Cox's principal, Dr Guggenheim, witheringly labels Max as 'one of the worst students we've got'; 'A Quick One, While He's Away' by the Who (1966), also in *Rushmore*, when Max unleashes a swarm of bees into Herman's hotel room; and 'The Way I Feel Inside' by the Zombies (1965) in *The Life Aquatic with Steve Zissou*, when Ned's coffin is cast into the sea, accompanied by Rod Argent's mournful lyrics and Colin Blunstone's understated vocals and organ arrangement, fitting for a funeral. Anderson's musical taste may be anachronistic, but his ability to choose the ideal earworm always produces a satisfying intertextual resonance.

TOP: UK 7" vinyl pressing of the Rolling Stones' 1968 single 'Street Fighting Man'.

BOTTOM: UK 7" sleeve of the Creation's 1966 single 'Making Time', issued in 1977.

OPPOSITE: *Solidarité*: A French student raises a defiant fist during the May '68 protests in Paris (top). Mr Fox salutes the enigmatic Wolf, aka *Canis lupus* (bottom).

A WELL-RESPECTED MAN

When discussing Anderson's auditory prowess, it would be remiss not to mention his longtime music supervisor Randall Poster, who has been sourcing songs for film and television for over 25 years. Poster began his career in 1995 when director Larry Clark approached him to produce the soundtrack for his debut feature, *Kids*. Today, Poster is one of the most sought-after supervisors in the industry, having overseen the curation and clearance of music for almost 200 productions, including films by Todd Haynes, Richard Linklater and Martin Scorsese. Anderson and Poster first met during post-production on *Bottle Rocket*, and they have worked together ever since.

In 2015, when describing his job to *WIPO Magazine*, Poster clarified:

> What I do in the process of making a movie depends on its inherent musical character. Some movies have a very strong and dynamic on-camera musical element with actors or musicians performing on camera; but for others, the challenge is to identify the right musical sound for the film.

Reflecting on his successful collaborations with Anderson a year earlier in an interview with *Vice*, he said, 'I think one of the reasons why the work Wes and I have done together on the music side of things has been as potent as it has been, is that we spend a lot of time between movies thinking about the music.'

ABOVE: The Kinks posing in the gardens near Charing Cross, London in 1964.

OPPOSITE: Anderson and Randall Poster attending the closing night screening of *Isle of Dogs* at the 2018 SXSW Festival.

ANDERSON'S MUSICAL TASTE MAY BE ANACHRONISTIC, BUT HIS ABILITY TO CHOOSE THE IDEAL EARWORM ALWAYS PRODUCES A SATISFYING INTERTEXTUAL RESONANCE

'ALL WE WANT TO DO IS TO BE WITH ONE ANOTHER ALL THE TIME,
WE THOUGHT THAT MEANT GETTING MARRIED. DOESN'T IT?' – DANIEL

OPPOSITE: To love and
to cherish: Ornshaw
officiates a mock wedding
ceremony for Daniel and
Melody (top). Sam and
Suzy tie the knot with
a Khaki Scout troop in
attendance in *Moonrise
Kingdom* (bottom).

PART 4
Melody

(Waris Hussein, 1971)

Anderson has attributed François Truffaut's *L'argent de poche* (*Small Change*, 1976) with providing the initial creative spark for *Moonrise Kingdom*, but he has also stated that, while writing the script, he watched two British films that heavily informed the tone of his preteen romance: Ken Loach's *Black Jack* (1979) and Waris Hussein's *Melody*. Anderson described the latter film as 'a forgotten, inspiring gem' around the time of its Blu-ray release in 2017. Originally marketed in the UK as *S.W.A.L.K.* (an acronym of the phrase 'sealed with a loving kiss;' a message traditionally written on the envelopes of love letters by British schoolchildren), *Melody* failed to strike a chord with Western audiences upon its initial theatrical release but was a surprise box-office smash in Japan and has since earned cult status around the world.

Melody was the debut screenplay of the late, great Alan Parker, who went on to have a successful career as a filmmaker, directing such cult classics as *Bugsy Malone* (1976) and *Birdy* (1984). *Melody*'s soft-centred, Bee Gees-soundtracked story revolves around school-age sweethearts Daniel (Mark Lester) and Melody (Tracy Hyde), who fall in love and decide to get married over the course of a few months. The film starts out as a sort of bromance between Daniel and his scampish classmate Ornshaw, played by Jack Wild, who previously appeared alongside Lester as the Artful Dodger in Carol Reed's *Oliver!* (1968); the pair are so fun to watch that it's no wonder they were cast in more or less

the same roles in *Melody* three years later. But everything changes when Daniel catches a glimpse of Melody in a ballet lesson. Suddenly, he no longer cares about hanging out with his mates after school. Melody is all that matters.

The influence of *Melody* on *Moonrise Kingdom* – the preteen romance between Sam Shakusky (Jared Gilman) and Suzy Bishop (Kara Hayward) – is hard to miss. Firstly, Daniel is part of the Boys' Brigade, a uniformed Christian youth organization not unlike the Khaki Scouts which Sam belongs to. However, while Sam is only too eager to show off the various merit badges he has earned, Daniel is much shyer and more self-effacing. In *Melody*'s opening scene, he admits that his smart appearance is all down to his mother, and that he doesn't really know what he's doing in the Brigade, much to the amusement of the other boys and the consternation of their captain. Yet they both demonstrate their worth to their would-be girlfriends: Daniel accompanies Melody in a tender rendition of 'Frère Jacques' on his cello; Sam impresses Suzy with his orienteering skills and all-round resourcefulness.

There are other, more superficial points of comparison: the way Sam first notices Suzy, through a gap in a clothes rail as she's applying her raven makeup backstage, is reminiscent of how Daniel experiences love at first sight, gazing at Melody through a window as she practises her pirouette (Anderson does something similar in *Rushmore* in the scene where Max stares at Miss Cross, played by Olivia

Williams, through a crack in a classroom door). And there's Edward Norton's schoolmasterish scout leader, who smokes and cusses and is constantly given the runaround by Sam, not unlike Daniel's teacher. More than anything, though, Anderson channels the joyful spirit of *Melody*, a film whose most captivating scenes — the exuberant sports day montage (shot by Parker as second unit director); Daniel and Melody frolicking through an overgrown cemetery, a sequence echoed in Sam and Suzy's hike through the woods — provide the emotional blueprint for *Moonrise Kingdom*.

Before they agree to elope, Daniel and Melody skip school and escape to the seaside, where they eat candy floss, build sandcastles and splash around in the shallows. They don't cut shapes on the sand quite like Sam and Suzy do during their beach campout, but Anderson owes a debt to Parker, Hussein and cinematographer Peter Suschitzky for the freeness with which they capture these playful, naturalistic images. The connective tissue between the films also extends to how the characters behave. Love does something strange to Sam, just as it does Daniel, whose determination to spend every moment with Melody turns him from a meek boy into a confident young man who is prepared to take the kind of risks he would never have taken before.

Youthful rebellion is not always about causing trouble or putting oneself in danger, though. It can be a harmless and even healthy part of growing up, as is largely the case in both *Melody* and *Moonrise Kingdom*. But when the school's headmaster (James Cossins) learns of Daniel and Melody's plan to wed, all-out anarchy ensues. A mob of dismayed teachers lead a chaotic pursuit of the couple, tracking them down at a disused railway arch where they are staging a mock ceremony, with Ornshaw serving as the officiant and the rest of the class acting as witnesses. After interrupting the vows and causing the children to scatter, the teachers are rounded upon, and one boy explodes the school minibus with a homemade bomb.

Both the impromptu nuptials and the riotous kids-vs-adults melee that cap off Hussein's film are evoked in *Moonrise Kingdom*'s stormy third act, pyrotechnics and all. During Fort Lebanon's annual summer Hullabaloo, Jason Schwartzman's Khaki Scout staffer agrees to preside over Sam and Suzy's union, as well as ensure their safe passage away from the camp. Just when the 'newlyweds' look set to sail off into the proverbial sunset, dark clouds gather and Sam is struck by lightning.

Anderson opts for a more grounded ending: Sam and Suzy's earnest act of defiance is ultimately short-lived, as they are finally apprehended and taken away by their respective guardians. In contrast, the very last shot of *Melody* shows Daniel and Melody disappearing over the horizon on a handcar, a fairy tale send-off that is charmingly at odds with the film's grey-skied view of early 1970s London.

THE INFLUENCE OF MELODY ON MOONRISE KINGDOM IS HARD TO MISS

LEFT: The official UK quad poster for Melody.

ABOVE: Daniel first sets eyes on Melody through a classroom door (top row). Anderson has copied this set-up in *Moonrise Kingdom*, when Sam introduces himself to Suzy backstage (second row) and in *Rushmore*, when Max spies Miss Cross teaching her class (third row).

In another *Moonrise Kingdom* scene influenced by *Melody*, Sam and Suzy enjoy a day at the beach (bottom right), much like Daniel and Melody (bottom left).

CHAPTER 2

FORBIDDEN LOVE

'MRS ROBINSON, IF YOU DON'T MIND MY SAYING SO,
THIS CONVERSATION IS GETTING A LITTLE STRANGE.'
– BENJAMIN BRADDOCK

OPPOSITE: Hello darkness
my old friend: Benjamin
appears to have the
weight of the world on
his shoulders (top), while
Max, too, is feeling blue
in *Rushmore* (bottom).

PART 1
The Graduate

(Mike Nichols, 1967)

When speaking to Rotten Tomatoes in 2012 about his all-time favourite films, Anderson named fellow countryman Mike Nichols as 'one of the most inventive directors that we've had,' citing his multi-Oscar-winning black comedy *Who's Afraid of Virginia Woolf?* (1966). Anderson admitted, however, that he didn't fall in love with the film the first time he saw it. Instead, it was Nichols' next effort that stole his heart. *The Graduate* follows a disaffected college grad named Benjamin Braddock (Dustin Hoffman), who has an affair with a married woman before becoming infatuated with her daughter during a long, listless summer back home in suburban Los Angeles. As subversive as it was successful, the film left an indelible mark on American cinema.

In *Rushmore* (1998), Anderson once again demonstrates his 'scavenger-hunt sensibility', as Matt Zoller Seitz has termed it, drawing from influences as wide-ranging as Chet Baker and *Barry Lyndon* (Stanley Kubrick, 1975), Charlie Brown and *Chinatown* (Roman Polanski, 1974), Jules Verne and *Jules et Jim* (François Truffaut, 1962). But it's *The Graduate* with which *Rushmore* shares most of its DNA, where Max Fischer (Jason Schwartzman) falls in love with an older woman, first grade teacher Rosemary Cross (Olivia Williams). This is immediately evident in the way the main characters are styled, with Max's school uniform – navy blazer, buttoned-down Oxford shirt, striped tie, slacks – clearly inspired by the preppy attire Benjamin wears at the start of *The Graduate*. Yet the films also have a more subtle, aqueous bond.

When he's not chasing around after Mrs Robinson (Anne Bancroft) or Elaine (Katharine Ross), Benjamin spends most of his free time floating in his parents' pool, drifting in a state of comfortable numbness. In one such scene, Mrs Braddock (Elizabeth Wilson) suggests inviting the entire Robinson family round to dinner, prompting an agonized Benjamin to put a halt to the conversation by flopping off his inflatable. Later, when he finally comes clean to Elaine about his fling with her mother, he looks like he's just been plunged into a vat of cold water: his eyes bleary, his clothes soaked through with rain and regret.

Similarly, *Rushmore* is awash with water-based symbolism, much of it borrowed from Nichols' film. There's the moment when Herman Blume (Bill Murray), a parent at Max's school and its main benefactor, jumps into the pool at his sons' birthday party and holds his breath underwater, just as Benjamin does at his 21st birthday party, weighed down by scuba diving equipment and his parents' expectations – both characters finding temporary sanctuary beneath the surface. While we're on the subject, in *Bottle Rocket* (1996), Luke Wilson's Anthony first locks eyes on Paraguayan maid Inez (Lumi Cavazos) from a motel pool, and their meet-cute continues during a late-night dip.

Although not quite for the same reasons as Benjamin, Max is also drowning. One of the most revealing scenes in *Rushmore* occurs early on when Max and Miss Cross feed the fish in the class aquarium. Both actors are positioned behind the row of tanks so that when they bend down for a closer look, it appears as if their heads are underwater. The shot echoes a scene in *The Graduate* where Benjamin, hiding from his own homecoming, is shown slumped dejectedly next to a fish tank (complete with miniature scuba diver) in his bedroom.

It's at this point that Mrs Robinson makes her move. She enters Benjamin's room claiming, somewhat unconvincingly, to be looking for the bathroom. She then lights a cigarette and asks what is troubling him before requesting – or rather insisting – that he drive her home. Despite putting up a mild protest, Benjamin acquiesces, only for Mrs Robinson to tease him by tossing the car keys into the fish tank, which he dutifully retrieves. He seems oblivious to the fact that her seduction of him has already begun. Similarly, Anderson uses the fish tank scene in *Rushmore* to establish a connection between Max and Miss Cross. It is here that they reveal they have each lost someone close to them.

The implications of these interactions are very different, but the upshot is the same: both Benjamin and Max are about to embark on a wildly inappropriate relationship with an adult woman. Of course, Benjamin does not appear to have much say in the matter. His graduation to manhood occurs with his full consent, but he could hardly be described as the instigator. In contrast, while Max boasts (untruthfully) about receiving a hand job from a fellow student's mother in the back of her Jaguar, Anderson never gives the impression that

Max's crush on Miss Cross will be reciprocated. This is not to say that Max gives up easily.

In a grand if somewhat foolhardy gesture, Max breaks ground on a marine observatory on school property without the permission of Dr Guggenheim (Brian Cox), resulting in him being kicked out of Rushmore Academy; a plot point inspired by co-writer Owen Wilson's own expulsion from high school for cheating on a geometry test. Max eventually returns to Rushmore after rustling up another half-baked romantic scheme. However, upon entering Miss Cross's classroom, he passes two removals men carrying out an empty fish tank – a sign that any faint hope he had of winning her over may have already vanished.

Anderson leaves things there as far as fish tanks are concerned, but Nichols has one last visual metaphor up his sleeve. At the end of *The Graduate*, Benjamin finishes with Mrs Robinson but fails to patch things up with Elaine, who by this point has found herself another suitor. As a last resort, Benjamin crashes Elaine's wedding in dramatic fashion. Finding the front doors to the church locked, he races up an adjacent stairwell and emerges in a viewing gallery overlooking the ceremony. When the camera cuts to Elaine's perspective, Benjamin appears scaled-down, dwarfed by the massive pane of glass separating him from his sweetheart. His raw emotion is on display for everyone to see.

FAR LEFT: The official US one-sheet poster for *The Graduate*.

LEFT: A rain-soaked Benjamin confesses all to an unsuspecting Elaine.

OPPOSITE: Anderson returned to his old alma mater for his second feature, replacing the St John's School sign (bottom) with one for his film's fictional academy (top).

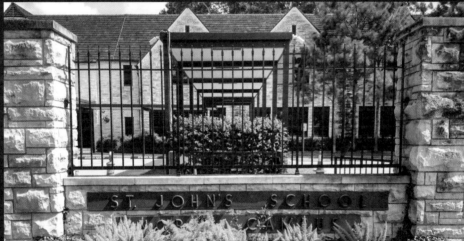

OLD SCHOOL TIES

Like many of the fictional settings used in Anderson's films, Rushmore Academy is an amalgam of various real-life establishments. Principal photography took place in Houston between November 1997 and February 1998, with Anderson's own prep school, St John's, doubling for the Rushmore campus. For the opening establishing shot, in which a set of navy-blue drapes are drawn to reveal the name of the academy and the title of the film, a small hedgerow was added beneath the fence to obscure the St John's emblem.

Other academic institutes featured in *Rushmore* include the Kinkaid School, North Shore High School (where Max premieres his play at the end of the film) and Lamar High School, where Anderson's father briefly attended, and which is situated across the street from St John's. Anderson and his production team transformed Lamar High School into Grover Cleveland High School, where Max enrols after his suspension from Rushmore. Another inspiration for Grover Cleveland was St Mark's, the Houston private school from which Owen Wilson was expelled.

OPPOSITE: Benjamin identifies with a sunken diver figurine in his bedroom fish tank (top), while Max and Miss Cross admire the occupants of a tank in the teacher's classroom (bottom).

RIGHT: One of several scenes of Benjamin going underwater to escape his mundane existence (top). Anderson has Herman match Benjamin's mood in *Rushmore* (middle), while in *The Royal Tenenbaums*, Royal, Ari and Uzi go for a more enjoyable dip during their grand day out (bottom).

'IT'S BEST NOT TO BE TOO MORAL. YOU CHEAT YOURSELF OUT OF TOO MUCH LIFE.' – MAUDE

OPPOSITE: Time to talk: A reluctant Harold meets with a psychiatrist at his mother's behest (top). In *Rushmore*, Max has a heart-to-heart with Dr. Guggenheim in the headmaster's office (bottom).

PART 2
Harold and Maude

(Hal Ashby, 1971)

'Whenever I am getting ready to make a movie,' Anderson told *GOOD Magazine* in 2008:

> I look at other movies I love in order to answer the same recurring question: How is this done, again? . . . Making a movie is very complicated, and it seems like kind of a miracle when it actually works out. Hal Ashby made five or six great movies in a row, and that seems to be practically unheard of . . . To me, they are some of the best movies ever made. Sometimes, like the opening scene and much of *Coming Home* (1978), they almost resemble documentaries. Sometimes, for instance in the cases of *Harold and Maude* and *Being There* (1979), they are quite surreal.

With its autumnal palette and existential themes, *Harold and Maude* has provided Anderson with a constant source of inspiration over the years. The film centres on a depressed, hearse-driving teenager named Harold (Bud Cort, who has a cameo in *The Life Aquatic with Steve Zissou* (2004) as bond company stooge Bill Ubell) and a bohemian septuagenarian full of bonhomie named Maude (Ruth Gordon) – an odd couple who discover they are soulmates. They meet at a stranger's funeral, where they have each come to contemplate their own mortality.

Death looms over the film. In the opening scene, Harold fastidiously puts a record on, writes a note, pins it to his lapel,

lights a candle, then steps onto a stool and pretends to hang himself – the first of many elaborate fake suicides he stages to antagonize his mother. The surrealness that Anderson is referring to stems from *Harold and Maude*'s gallows humour and offbeat tone, which, like Anderson's own films, are grounded in realism but are delightfully idiosyncratic at the same time.

In 1971, critics and audiences didn't quite know what to make of *Harold and Maude*. It didn't help that Paramount, apparently unsure how to market the film, released a promotional poster bearing only the title and top-billed credits. Negative press, such as A.D. Murphy's scathing critique in *Variety* that described the film as having 'all the fun and gaiety of a burning orphanage,' and Vincent Canby's review in the *New York Times* that labelled Cort and Gordon 'mismatched', 'creepy and off-putting', resulted in paltry box-office receipts. *Harold and Maude* didn't turn a profit until 1983, thanks to its wider availability on home video, but is now regarded as a cult classic and even one of the defining films of the era. It is emblematic of a time when filmmakers exerted much more creative control and were free to push boundaries by tackling taboo subject matter.

Being an unconventional romance about a young man and a much older woman, the Anderson film that *Harold and Maude* most resembles is *Rushmore*. Of course, Max is unsuccessful in his pursuit of Miss Cross, but like the protagonists of Ashby's film, both characters come to understand each other's perspectives on love and life. There is significant aural overlap too. While filming *Harold and Maude*, Ashby listened to the Cat Stevens album *Tea for the Tillerman* (1970) on repeat, even layering snippets of it over the dailies. When the director approached Stevens looking for a song for Maude to sing, he was offered two brand new, unrecorded tunes, 'Don't be Shy' (1970) and 'If You Want to Sing Out, Sing Out' (1970). Stevens also agreed to perform alternative versions of previously released material for the film. *Rushmore* features two Stevens songs on its soundtrack: 'Here Comes My Baby' (1967) and 'The Wind' (1971). The former is heard when Max asks Miss Cross if she might consider a strictly platonic relationship; the latter when Max flies a box kite at an airfield after being called a jerk, justifiably so, by eventual love interest Margaret Yang (Sara Tanaka).

Rushmore also includes several visual nods to *Harold and Maude*. The rather pathetic-looking Blume family portrait seen at the beginning of the film evokes, in its amateurishness and awkwardness, two paintings by Maude that she shows Harold. One is titled *The Rape of Rome*, in which she depicts herself being sexually assaulted by a swan, and the other is *Rainbow with Egg Underneath and an Elephant*, whose title speaks for itself. The swimming pool scene in *Harold and Maude*, which was directly inspired

by *The Graduate*, is similar to *Rushmore* in that both Harold and Herman are shown 'drowning'. Max's house is situated alongside a cemetery, a subtle nod to Harold's favourite pastime. And Max's heart-to-heart with Dr Guggenheim is almost identical in composition to the scene where Harold sits with a psychiatrist; both characters are turned slightly towards each other facing the camera.

Elsewhere, the shot of Harold and Maude cavorting on a hillside has a similar vibe to Sam (Jared Gilman) and Suzy's (Kara Hayward) uninhibited grooving in *Moonrise Kingdom* (2012). Additionally, the way the couple are filmed moving through the railcar in which Maude lives calls to mind *The Darjeeling Limited* (2007), which Anderson co-wrote with Roman Coppola and Jason Schwartzman, who is also a huge *Harold and Maude* fan. Reflecting on the making of *Rushmore*, Schwartzman revealed that his mother suggested he watch three films in preparation for playing Max: *The Graduate*, *Dog Day Afternoon* (Sidney Lumet, 1975) and *Harold and Maude*. 'From the second [*Harold and Maude*] started,' he said, 'my life as I knew it was over . . . *Harold and Maude*, to my 17-year-old mind, was a whole new place . . . my life just kind of made sense to me in a single moment. I felt not so bad.' For all its morbidness, *Harold and Maude* is ultimately a film about embracing the possibilities of living.

LEFT: The cover of Cat Stevens' original soundtrack album for *Harold and Maude* (left) and the cover of his 1970 studio album *Tea for the Tillerman* (right).

OPPOSITE: Bud Cort gets ready to act out one of Harold's elaborate fake suicides (top).

Maude shows Harold colourfully titled painting *The Rape of Rome* (bottom left); its amateurish style is aped in the Blume family portrait that appears during *Rushmore's* opening credits (bottom right).

'DON'T YOU SEE THAT YOU TWO TOGETHER
ARE DANGEROUS?' – HOWARD

OPPOSITE: Doomed lovers: Howard keeps a watchful eye on his wife Mary and her caddish admirer Steven (top). M. Gustave plays a more supportive role in Zero and Agatha's romantic relationship in *The Grand Budapest Hotel* (bottom).

PART 3
The Passionate Friends

(David Lean, 1949)

David Lean's *The Passionate Friends* tells the story of Mary Justin (Ann Todd) and Steven Stratton (Trevor Howard), two star-crossed lovers whose on-and-off romance is recounted through a series of flashbacks spanning almost a decade. Lean based the film on H.G. Wells' novel of the same name, first published in 1913, but in adapting it for the screen, he and co-writer Stanley Haynes crucially changed the point of view. In the book, the first-person narrator is Steven, but in the film, Mary is the one who reminisces about their relationship. Ironically, during the filming of *The Passionate Friends* in the summer of 1948, Lean, then married to the actor Kay Walsh, began an affair with Todd.

While *The Passionate Friends* may not be as highly regarded as Lean's earlier romantic drama *Brief Encounter* (1945), it remains a gripping and gorgeous study of human connection that has withstood the test of time. Anderson listed it as one of his favourite lockdown rewatches in a May 2020 interview with the *New York Times*, along with George Cukor's *What Price Hollywood?* (1932), George Stevens' *Alice Adams* (1935), John Ford's *The Long Voyage Home* (1940), John Huston's *Beat the Devil* (1953) and Spike Lee's *Do the Right Thing* (1989). Of these films, *The Passionate Friends* has had the most apparent influence on Anderson.

For starters, Ralph Fiennes' M. Gustave, the genteel protagonist of *The Grand Budapest Hotel* (2014), shares more than a hint of resemblance with Steven Stratton and is himself no stranger to an indiscreet liaison. Both men come

from lower middle-class backgrounds – one a college lecturer, the other a hotel manager – and disguise this fact with their mannerisms. They are deeply sentimental, devilishly cavalier and prone to reciting poetry. Yet while Steven quotes from John Keats' 'Endymion', M. Gustave's flowery, oft-interrupted verses are entirely fabricated; it's never made clear whether the author is him or someone else within the world of the film. And while M. Gustave is usually seen wearing his hotel uniform, it's easy to imagine him sporting a paisley ascot and wide-collared shirt like Stratton's on an off-season sojourn.

Characterization and costume aren't the only points of comparison. Although *The Grand Budapest Hotel*'s concertinaed narrative structure was inspired by the writings of Stefan Zweig, to be discussed in Chapter 8, *The Passionate Friends* uses a similar flashback-within-a-flashback framing device. Lean's film opens at a luxurious lakeside resort near the Swiss Alps called Hotel Splendide, where Mary and Steven reunite by chance on the balcony of their adjoining rooms. That evening, Mary lies on her bed in the dark and recalls a fateful New Year's Eve party from nine years prior. Back in the present, they take a boat across the lake, catch a cable car and enjoy a picnic high up in the mountains. Although they do not yet realize it, this is as close to heaven as they will ever be together.

Mary's wealthy investor husband, Howard (Claude Rains), brings her back down to earth. He views marriage strictly as a matter of convenience, something practical and transactional, and scoffs at Steven's idea of love, contending that it 'makes big demands' of 'nearness, belonging, fulfilment and priority over everything else'. In a frosty meeting between the two men, Howard insists that what Steven can offer Mary is not what she really wants and promises to do everything within his power to keep them apart. Rejecting Howard's 'cold, bloodless banker's point of view,' Steven pleads his case: 'We're human beings, not joint stock companies, and you can't move us around as if we were.'

Being set in the 1940s, *The Passionate Friends* is inevitably shrouded by the fog of war, just as *The Grand Budapest Hotel* is. At one point, Howard further denounces the notion of romanticism by equating it to the rise of fascism in Nazi Germany:

Personally, Stratton, I think there is a fault in the Teutonic mind, which shows up whenever they have access to great power. Sort of . . . romantic hysteria. Well, perhaps not romantic, but a hysteria anyway, which seems to convert them from a collection of sober, intelligent, rather sentimental individuals, into a dangerous mob. A mob which can believe that a big enough lie is not a lie at all . . . but truth.

In Anderson's film, M. Gustave is portrayed as both vain and needy, but also as a man of ethics and integrity. In contrast to Howard's belittling and divisive language, he espouses acceptance and tolerance in response to the authoritarian regime that encroaches upon the cosmopolitan Republic of Zubrowka, named after a popular brand of Polish vodka. In laying out his principles to the rest of the hotel staff, he remarks: 'Rudeness is merely an expression of fear. People fear they won't get what they want. The most dreadful and unattractive person only needs to be loved and they will open up like a flower.' At this moment, M. Gustave not only reveals his own basic faith in humanity but also Anderson's.

To Lean's and Rains' immense credit, we end up empathizing with Howard, even when he threatens to destroy Mary by filing for divorce. He is, after all, a victim in this story, guilty only of not being able to offer Mary what her heart desires – a hard truth he must ultimately come to terms with. In the end, it is Howard and M. Gustave who are most closely allied. While one man resigns himself to staying in a loveless marriage, the other eats his meals alone, despite claiming to have many intimate acquaintances. Both maintain mutually beneficial relationships built on superficial pleasures such as sex and money, thereby denying themselves true happiness.

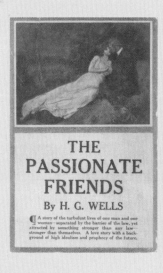

FAR LEFT: First edition book cover for H.G. Wells' 1913 novel *The Passionate Friends*.

LEFT: The official US quad poster for *The Passionate Friends*.

OPPOSITE: Steven seduces Mary during their romantic tryst in the Swiss Alps (top); the former was a key inspiration for M. Gustave, who is introduced as having a similar way with (much older) women (bottom).

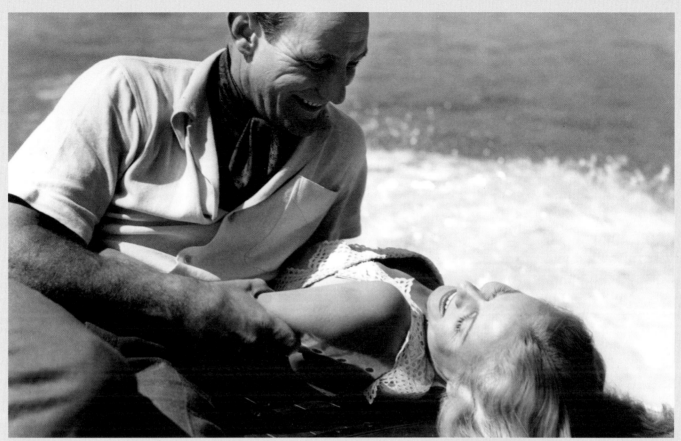

THE COUNTESS AND THE PAINTER

The family name of Tilda Swinton's wealthy dowager in *The Grand Budapest Hotel,* Desgoffe und Taxis, is a reference to the nineteenth-century French still-life painter Blaise Alexandre Desgoffe, whose style was emulated by British artist Michael Taylor in the creation of *Boy with Apple* for the film. Anderson invented a backstory for the faux Renaissance-era prop, attributing it to the fictional Johannes Van Hoytl the Younger, an 'extremely unprolific' and financially unsuccessful artist who 'nevertheless produced perhaps a dozen of the finest portraits of the period'. The art critic Jonathan Jones has described *Boy with Apple* as 'a priceless art history in-joke'.

In the film, Swinton's character is more commonly referred to as Madame D., evoking the title of Max Ophüls' romantic drama, *The Earrings of Madame de . . .* (1953), which Anderson called 'a perfect film' in a piece for the *Criterion Collection. Madame de . . .* has a certain narrative likeness to *The Grand Budapest Hotel,* as it tells of an upper-class woman who, in order to pay off her debts, sells a pair of earrings gifted to her by her husband on their wedding day, thus setting off a chain of tragic events.

OPPOSITE: The painting *Boy with Apple* by British artist Michael Taylor (left), who took inspiration from various still-lifes by the nineteenth-century French painter Blaise Alexandre Desgoffe, such as *A Still Life with Peaches, Plums and Cherries* (right).

ABOVE: The titular Madame de contemplates giving away her prized earrings (top); the character is the namesake of Tilda Swinton's wealthy dowager in *The Grand Budapest Hotel* (bottom).

'NO MATTER WHAT HAPPENS TO US, I NEVER WANT
TO LEAVE YOUR SIDE.' – OSAN

OPPOSITE: Sliding doors:
A typical static shot used
by Mizoguchi, where
characters are blocked
around and framed
by doorways (top).
Anderson's style lends
itself to a similar technique,
as seen in *Moonrise
Kingdom* when Mrs Bishop
calls for Suzy through
a megaphone (bottom).

PART 4
A Story from Chikamatsu

(Kenji Mizoguchi, 1954)

Isle of Dogs (2018), Anderson's most overtly Japan-inspired film to date, sparked a heated debate about cultural appropriation and the othering of Japanese and East Asian customs by Western filmmakers for predominantly Western audiences. Without wishing to ignore or inflame that particular discourse, it is important to note that Anderson has always been open about his affection for Japanese cinema and several of the country's most revered filmmakers, namely Yasujirō Ozu, Hayao Miyazaki and Akira Kurosawa. These directors are discussed in Chapters 3, 6 and 7, respectively. In a 2018 interview with *JAPAN Forward*, Anderson admitted that 'not only are my films influenced by Japanese cinema, but I think so is my idea of what a movie director is'.

One Japanese film on Anderson's *New York Times* lockdown viewing list was *A Story from Chikamatsu*, a late-career masterwork from Kenji Mizoguchi, who directed a staggering 99 films from 1923 until his death in 1956. Released in the West under the spoilerific alternative title *The Crucified Lovers*, this adaptation of a traditional *jōruri* (sung narrative) stage play by Chikamatsu Monzaemon, who is often hailed as Japan's greatest classical dramatist, concerns a rich but miserly grand scroll master named Ishun (Eitarō Shindō) who wrongly accuses his wife, Osan (Kyōko Kagawa), and his assistant, Mohei (Kazuo Hasegawa), of adultery – a crime punishable by death in Edo-era Japan.

In fact, it is Ishun who is guilty of being unfaithful. Late one evening, he sneaks into the bedroom of one of his maids, Otama (Yôko Minamida), and pressures her for sex. Aware that she is powerless but desperate to maintain her dignity, Otama lies about being engaged to Mohei in the hope that Ishun will lose interest and leave her alone. But Ishun is unaware that Osan, knowing her husband to be ungenerous and unsympathetic, has also turned to Mohei for help with a small but urgent financial matter.

When Mohei is caught attempting to steal from the print shop by forging an invoice with his boss's insignia, Otama leaps to his defence, causing Ishun to banish his supposed romantic rival. Mohei returns later that night to thank Otama for standing up for him, only to find Osan waiting to confront Ishun about his infidelity in her place. Another worker catches the pair in what looks like a compromising position, and Ishun jumps to conclusions. He urges Osan to commit *seppuku*, a form of ritual suicide by disembowelment, to preserve his honour. But she refuses and follows Mohei in fleeing the household in disgrace.

A Story from Chikamatsu tackles a range of complex issues, including the inner struggle between desire and duty, the corrupting influence of money and power, and the historical suppression of women in Japanese society. Despite the film's weighty themes and melodramatic overtones, however, Mizoguchi manages to demonstrate a remarkable lightness of touch. The result is a period film with a progressive message and distinctly modernist tone. Cinematographer Kazuo Miyagawa, whose other credits include several films directed by Kurosawa and one by Ozu, stayed true to the source material by employing innovative lighting and framing techniques designed to simulate the experience of watching a *bunraku* (puppet theatre) performance. The specific combination of medium wide shots and fixed camera placement creates a physical distance from the characters, a technique that Anderson has similarly put to good use.

Mizoguchi's prolific career spanned the silent era and the advent of sound through to the fall of Imperial Japan and the subsequent American occupation. Over time, he evolved from a workmanlike director of commercially driven studio pictures, the majority of which are now sadly lost, into a bona fide auteur of challenging, contemplative dramas that connected Japan's distant feudal past to its difficult post-war reconstruction. His later films, particularly *The Life of Oharu* (1952), *Ugetsu* (1953), *A Story from Chikamatsu* and *Sansho the Bailiff* (1954), are heart-rending, thought-provoking tales of domestic strife in which characters are separated, usually against their will, and made to suffer in their quest for survival.

Anderson and Mizoguchi share many of the same dramatic impulses. While Anderson generally avoids overt social commentary – something Mizoguchi became increasingly known for over the course of his career – he foregrounds emotional trauma and romantic entanglement in much the same way as the Japanese director. The pining schoolboys, estranged relatives and lovers on the lam that occupy *Rushmore*, *The Royal Tenenbaums* (2001) and *Moonrise Kingdom* are all to some extent shaped by their surroundings; the moral dilemmas they confront are symptomatic of broader social conflicts and constraints, as well as individual family struggles.

Like many of Mizoguchi's later films, *A Story from Chikamatsu* ends in tragedy. After absconding together, Mohei and Osan row out to the middle of Lake Biwa on the outskirts of Kyoto with the intention of carrying out a double suicide. But Mohei's confession of his true feelings for Osan completely alters her outlook: moments earlier, she was ready to die; now, she has every reason to live. This beautiful and intimate scene, captured in a long, unbroken take, also serves to underscore the couple's predicament – they are, quite literally, in the same boat, cut adrift from a world they know they can never return to.

Mohei and Osan's sudden mutual declaration can therefore be seen as them implicitly coming to an agreement over their shared destiny. When they are eventually captured and brought back to Kyoto to be executed, they are paraded through the centre of the city on horseback; their bodies bound together, their hands tightly clasped in a tender, defiant public display of their undying love.

DESPITE THE FILM'S WEIGHTY THEMES AND MELODRAMATIC OVERTONES, MIZOGUCHI MANAGES TO DEMONSTRATE A REMARKABLE LIGHTNESS OF TOUCH

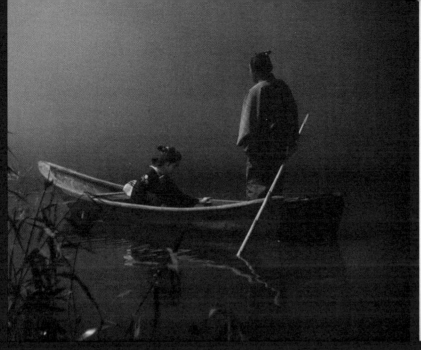

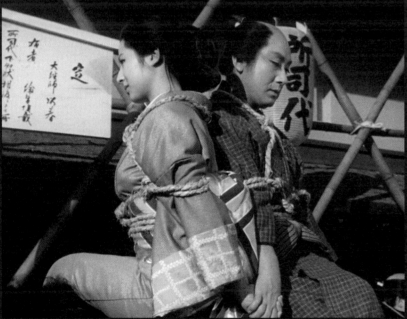

OPPOSITE: Illustration
of the seventeenth- to
eighteenth-century
Japanese dramatist
Chikamatsu Monzaemon.

ABOVE: After tragedy is
seemingly averted on the
still waters of Lake Biwa
(top left), Mohei and Osan
are symbolically lashed
together and carried to
their death (bottom left).

The official Japanese
theatrical poster for A
Story from Chikamatsu
(top right).

Anderson has cited Kenji
Mizoguchi (bottom right)
as one of his favourite
Japanese filmmakers.

CHAPTER 3

FAMILY VALUES

'AGAINST SO HOMESPUN A BACKGROUND,
THE MAGNIFICENCE OF THE AMBERSONS WAS AS CONSPICUOUS
AS A BRASS BAND AT A FUNERAL.' – NARRATOR

OPPOSITE: Table manners: The dinner scene featuring the extended Amberson family (top) provided Anderson with a handy reference for his own study of a dysfunctional upper-class family in *The Royal Tenenbaums* (bottom).

PART 1
The Magnificent Ambersons

(Orson Welles, 1942)

Anderson relocated to New York City shortly after the release of *Rushmore* (1998), and from the moment he arrived, he knew he wanted to make a film there. He soon decided that the film should be about an eccentric family living in a large house somewhere in Manhattan; naturally, he turned to *The Magnificent Ambersons* for inspiration. Orson Welles' Gilded Age drama, based on the 1918 Pulitzer Prize-winning novel by Newton Booth Tarkington (after whom Anderson named the theatre in *Asteroid City*, 2023), depicts a dynasty in decline in a semi-fictionalized turn-of-the-century Indianapolis. The film abounds with absent parents, spoiled children, doomed lovers and characters generally clinging to past glories – all archetypes that will be familiar to Anderson's fans.

Despite being set in the American Midwest, Welles' film provided the blueprint for much of *The Royal Tenenbaums* (2001). The Ambersons' grand Victorian mansion, the look of which was partly inspired by Edward Hopper's 1925 painting *House by the Railroad*, closely resembles the Tenenbaum's red-brick townhouse. Anderson found the house for his film while driving around Harlem in the spring of 2000 with his friend, record producer George Drakoulias, and his assistant, Will Sweeney. Although Anderson has described this as a lucky accident, his choice of location may have been subconsciously influenced by his feeling towards Welles, whom he has described as 'one of my very favourite directors' and 'one of my heroes'.

It is no coincidence that both films open with exterior shots of these imposing edifices, establishing at once the primary setting and the elevated social status of the respective occupants. The Tenenbaum residence (officially known as the Charles H. Tuttle mansion in real life after its former owner, a prominent lawyer and politician who ran for state governor against Franklin D. Roosevelt in 1930), is situated in the Hamilton Heights neighbourhood. The four-storey property was designed in the Flemish Revival style by Adolph Hoak and constructed in 1899 by a prominent developer named Jacob D. Butler. Its corner tower, stepped gable, carved mantelpieces and parquet floors instantly identify it as belonging to a bygone era, much like the titular family of Anderson's film.

As fate would have it, when Anderson dropped a note through the door enquiring about the house's availability, the new owner was in the process of drawing up plans to renovate it and agreed to delay the work until after principal photography had been completed. Anderson struck a deal to rent the entire place for six months and, with the help of his illustrator brother Eric, spent several months prior to filming planning exactly how he wanted each room to look. The director also worked closely with production designer David Wasco and set decorator Sandy Reynolds-Wasco, furnishing the house to match the exotic tastes of matriarch Etheline Tenenbaum (Anjelica Huston), as well as the personalities of the three Tenenbaum children: Chas (Ben Stiller), Richie (Luke Wilson) and Margot (Gwyneth Paltrow).

They kept the period character and added antique Turkish rugs, trophy cabinets, vintage typewriters and computers, and traditional African masks (presumably acquired on one of Etheline's archaeological trips). Anderson's obsessive attention to detail when it comes to interior design cannot be overstated. The screenplay for

The Royal Tenenbaums describes the walls of Margot's bedroom as 'red, with little running zebras painted all over them'. According to a 2001 article published in the *Observer*, Anderson sourced the distinctive pattern from an Italian restaurant called Gino's on the Upper East Side, which had it custom made in the 1940s.

BELOW AND RIGHT: The zebra-print wallpaper seen in Margot's bedroom (below) is a replica of a design once found in New York restaurant institution Gino of Capri (right), which Anderson frequented during filming.

ABOVE: The Amberson mansion (top left) forms the centrepiece of Welles' film, much like the stately New York residence (top right) in Anderson's film. Anderson further emulates Welles in the scene where Royal remonstrates with Margot on a staircase (middle and bottom right), in a manner reminiscent of Fanny and George's heated exchanges (middle and bottom left).

THE ENTIRE HOUSE
CAN BE VIEWED
AS A SYMBOL OF
THEIR ARRESTED
DEVELOPMENT

Nostalgia is a key aspect of Anderson's film, and it's telling that, when Chas, Margot and Richie return to the family home, it appears virtually unchanged from the one they knew growing up – a creaking monument to their squandered talent. They feel as much a part of the furniture as their father Royal's (Gene Hackman) prized boar's head and look just as uncomfortable when they are put back on display after years of being neglected. Indeed, the entire house can be viewed as a symbol of their arrested development, one whose rose-pink walls hold a huge amount of family history and personal trauma.

The Magnificent Ambersons also centres on a once proud and prosperous family that seems increasingly out of step with the modern world. The film follows Isabel Amberson (Dolores Costello), a wealthy socialite who marries local businessman Wilbur Minafer (Don Dillaway), despite secretly being in love with an eligible bachelor named Eugene Morgan (Joseph Cotten). Years later, a now-widowed Eugene and Isabel attempt to start up a belated romance, but they are ultimately thwarted by Wilbur's sister Fanny (Agnes Moorehead) and Isabel's only son George (Tim Holt), both of whom have desires on the considerable Amberson-Minafer fortune.

Welles uses the house to convey the anxieties, insecurities and obsolescence of the main characters. In one of his trademark end-credit sequences, he recites the names of set decorator Al Fields and set designer Mark-Lee Kirk over images of an ornate armchair and an architectural drawing. Between them, Fields and Kirk dressed the house with crystal chandeliers, stained glass windows and an imperial staircase that was so expensive to construct that RKO, the film's production company, chose to keep it for future productions rather than dismantle it. The staircase plays a pivotal role in the film: it's where Fanny and George conspire and clash on multiple occasions. The high-low angle framing of one such scene is replicated in *The Royal Tenenbaums* when Royal squabbles with Chas and later when he confronts Margot over her infidelity.

Another similarity between *The Magnificent Ambersons* and Anderson's film is the presence of an unnamed narrator. Welles himself begins the story with a seemingly trivial yet revealing piece of information about the eponymous family.

The cadence, rhythm and tone of his opening line, 'The magnificence of the Ambersons began in 1873', are matched by Alec Baldwin during his introductory statement, 'Royal Tenenbaum bought the house on Archer Avenue in the winter of his 35th year.' Still, as the late filmmaker and sometime Welles mentee Peter Bogdanovich noted in the *Guardian* in 2001, Anderson's vision 'is as uniquely (and recognizably) his as Welles's'.

OPPOSITE: The US first edition cover of the 1951 novel *The Catcher in the Rye* (left) by one of Anderson's literary heroes, J.D. Salinger (right).

LEFT: The official US theatrical poster for *The Magnificent Ambersons*.

BELOW: Orson Welles behind the camera on the set of *The Magnificent Ambersons*.

HEART OF GLASS

With themes of adventure, alienation and the loss of innocence, J.D. Salinger's *The Catcher in the Rye* is the clearest literary touchstone for Anderson's early films. However, it's Salinger's Glass Family stories that have had the most prolonged impact. Centring around a cast of recurring characters who are alternately described as highly eccentric, gifted and knowledgeable – none of which guarantees their happiness or success – the saga was originally serialized in the *New Yorker* between 1948 and 1965 with the exception of 'Down at Dinghy', published in *Harper*'s in 1949, which notably features Beatrice 'Boo Boo' Glass who marries a Mr Tannenbaum. On the occasion of Salinger's death in 2010, Anderson reflected in the *New Yorker*:

'I remembered this passage from the F. Scott Fitzgerald story "The Freshest Boy":

"He had contributed to the events by which another boy was saved from the army of the bitter, the selfish, the neurasthenic and the unhappy. It isn't given to us to know those rare moments when people are wide open and the lightest touch can wither or heal. A moment too late and we can never reach them any more in this world. They will not be cured by our most efficacious drugs or slain with our sharpest swords."

. . . and it occurred to me that more than everything else – more than all the things in his stories that I have been inspired by and imitated and stolen to the best of my abilities – *this* describes my experience of the works of J.D. Salinger.'

'ALL OF LIFE IS LIKE A RHYTHM. BIRTH, DEATH. DAY, NIGHT. HAPPINESS, SORROW. MEETING, PARTING.' – AMAL

OPPOSITE: Through the looking glasses: The opera glasses that provide Charulata with a window to the outside world (top) are a recurring reference throughout Anderson's filmography, most notably in the form of Suzy's binoculars in *Moonrise Kingdom* (bottom).

PART 2
Charulata

(*The Lonely Wife*, Satyajit Ray, 1964)

Widely regarded as one of the most important filmmakers of the twentieth century, Satyajit Ray was the first Indian director to win an Oscar, receiving an honorary statuette shortly before his death in 1992 for his 'rare mastery of the art of motion pictures'. Upon accepting the award, he remarked: 'The most distinctive feature [of my films] is that they are deeply rooted in Bengal; in Bengali culture, mannerisms and mores. What makes them universal in appeal is that they are about human beings.'

Despite Ray's relative obscurity across India as a whole, where Hindi-language Bollywood movies, followed by Tamil and Telugu productions, traditionally enjoy the largest audience shares, Ray has long been revered by his peers both at home and abroad. Martin Scorsese recalled to the *Washington Post* in 2002 that seeing Ray's debut feature, *Pather Panchali* (*Song of the Little Road*, 1955), on television as a teenager made him see the world differently, while Akira Kurosawa once said of his longtime friend and contemporary: 'Not to have seen the cinema of Ray means existing in the world without seeing the sun or the moon.'

Anderson's own introduction to Ray occurred at a similar age to Scorsese when he rented a copy of *Teen Kanya* (1961), also known as *Three Daughters*, on Betamax at his local video store in Houston while still in high school. His love of Ray's films, as well as Louis Malle's seven-part TV documentary series *Phantom India* (1969) and Jean Renoir's *The River* (1951), a coming-of-age story set on the banks of the Ganges, eventually led to a trip to India with Roman Coppola and Jason Schwartzman, which in turn led to them making a film there. It was Anderson's first to be set and produced outside the US.

Commenting on *The Darjeeling Limited*'s (2007) Ray connection, Anderson told the English-language Rajasthan newspaper the *Statesman* in 2007: 'He is the reason I came here, but his films have also inspired all my other movies in different ways . . . His films feel like novels to me. He draws you very close to his characters, and his stories are almost always about people going through a major internal transition.' *The Darjeeling Limited* is dedicated to Ray and, unsurprisingly, it borrows heavily from his work. If you look closely, you'll even notice a portrait of the director hanging on the wall of one of the train's carriages.

In *Nayak* (*The Hero*, 1966), the sharp-suited protagonist is repeatedly shown smoking in transit, while *Aranyer Din Ratri* (*Days and Nights in the Forest*, 1970) follows a group of friends escaping the hustle and bustle of Kolkata for a weekend in the country – an eventful excursion from which they return transformed and more tightly bonded than before. At the end of *The Darjeeling Limited*, the Whitman brothers leg it after a train, evoking the poignant moment in *Pather Panchali* when two children dash through a field to greet a passing steam engine. The train scenes in Anderson's film were shot on a specially designed locomotive travelling across Northwest India from Jodhpur to Jaisalmer through

the heart of the Thar desert; the same region where Ray filmed *Sonar Kella* (*The Golden Fortress*) in 1974.

Then there's *Charulata* (*The Lonely Wife*), which Anderson has described as one of Ray's 'most beautiful films'. It concerns a young upper-class woman named Charulata (Madhabi Mukherjee) who is married to a neglectful newspaper editor, Umapada (Shyamal Ghoshal). She spends her days confined to a palatial, impersonal house in colonial Kolkata, walled in by a patriarchal system designed to stifle her aspirations and desires. We first see Charulata fretfully peering at the outside world through a pair of opera glasses, a sequence of first-person POV shots mimicked by Anderson in *Moonrise Kingdom* (2012). But this is a story of self-discovery and self-emancipation.

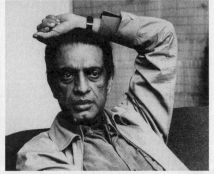

OPPOSITE: Satyajit Ray lining up a shot on the set of *Pather Panchali*.

ABOVE: A portrait of Ray is seen hanging in the cabin of the Whitman brothers' train carriage in *The Darjeeling Limited* (top); Ray photographed striking a similar pose (bottom right).

Anderson's film contains numerous references to other films by Ray, with Peter in *The Darjeeling Limited* (middle) seemingly channelling the protagonist of *The Hero*, aka *Nayak* (bottom left).

THE DARJEELING LIMITED IS DEDICATED TO RAY AND, UNSURPRISINGLY, IT BORROWS HEAVILY FROM HIS WORK

LEFT: The binocular effect seen throughout Ray's film (top) is mimicked by Anderson in several of his films, including *Moonrise Kingdom* (middle) and *Fantastic Mr. Fox* (bottom).

Over the course of the film, Charulata falls in love with her cousin-in-law, Amal (Soumitra Chatterjee), finally breaking out of her gilded cage.

In *The Darjeeling Limited*, Anderson likewise probes the emotional and physical boundaries that exist between the members of a family. The eponymous train represents the liminal space that the Whitmans – Francis (Owen Wilson), Jack (Jason Schwartzman) and Peter (Adrien Brody) – inhabit as they continue to mourn their father's death one year after his passing. Anderson's decision to use this compact and kinetic setting as the film's central motif was undoubtedly inspired by Ray, who harnessed the symbolic power of trains in The Apu Trilogy (*Pather Panchali; Aparajito*, 1956; *The World of Apu*, 1959), *Nayak* and *Sonar Kella*, among other films. However, just like in *Charulata*, it is only when the Whitmans step beyond their luxurious yet restrictive surroundings that they begin to build trust and a deeper connection with each other; their reconciliation sparked by a family tragedy that reminds them of their own. While Francis brings Jack and Peter to India in search of their estranged mother (Anjelica Huston), the journey is ultimately more important than the destination.

As a self-styled Renaissance man, Ray not only wrote and directed but also scored every one of his films after 1960's *Devi* (*The Goddess*). Along with songs by popular Western artists such as the Kinks and the Rolling Stones, *The Darjeeling Limited*'s soundtrack features a handful of original Ray compositions, as well as musical excerpts from the India-set Merchant-Ivory productions *The Householder* (1963), *Shakespeare Wallah* (1965) and *Bombay Talkie* (1970), all of which Ray had a significant influence on.

The soothing instrumental 'Charu's Theme' from *Charulata* appears several times in *The Darjeeling Limited*: first when Jack introduces himself to, and swiftly proceeds to fuck, 'sweet lime' stewardess Rita (Amara Karan); and later when they say goodbye after the brothers are kicked off the train for brawling among themselves. In a further echo of *Charulata*, Rita leans out of her cabin window and asks Jack tearfully, 'What's wrong with you?' Jack replies, 'Let me think about that,' before adding, 'Thanks for using me.' Rita takes a deep breath and sighs, 'You're welcome,' bringing their brief, romantically unfulfilling fling to its inevitable end.

RIGHT: The official Indian poster for *Charulata*.

FAR RIGHT: The young protagonists of *Pather Panchali* rush to greet a passing train; this was the first film by Ray that Anderson saw.

'I'M SURPRISED HOW CHILDREN CHANGE . . .
A MARRIED DAUGHTER IS LIKE A STRANGER.' – SHUKICHI

OPPOSITE: Sleep on it: The intimate framing that Ozu employs to depict characters resting (top) is echoed when Peter is shown dozing aboard the Darjeeling Limited (bottom).

PART 3
Tokyo Story

(Yasujirō Ozu, 1953)

Like many of Yasujirō Ozu's later films, *Tokyo Story* explores generational tensions within a conventional family structure, specifically between parents and their children. The film's simple narrative is set against a backdrop of rapid industrial development and social change, a thinly veiled metaphor for the complicated relationship between traditional and modern values in post-war Japan. Ozu returned to this theme throughout his career, most notably in *Late Spring* (1949), *Equinox Flower* (1958), *Good Morning* (1959) and *An Autumn Afternoon* (1962).

Tokyo Story follows Shukichi (Chishû Ryû) and Tomi (Chieko Higashiyama), an elderly couple who visit their children in the big city, leaving their tranquil seaside hometown for the first time in their lives. Upon their arrival in Tokyo, they discover that their eldest son Koichi (Sô Yamamura), a paediatrician, and daughter Shige (Haruko Sugimura), who runs a beauty salon with her husband, have little time for them. It's not that Koichi and Shige no longer care about their parents, but their priorities have shifted: both are portrayed as hard-working, free-willed and preoccupied with their own busy lives.

The Royal Tenenbaums sees gruff patriarch Royal engineer an impromptu family reunion for entirely selfish reasons. His revelation to estranged wife Etheline that he is dying of cancer leads him to return to the family pile, along with all their children. Back under one roof for the first time in many years, the Tenenbaums quickly fall back into old habits and reignite past feuds. Despite being in such close proximity, the distance between them is stark. Gradually, however, Tenenbaums and non-Tenenbaums alike make peace with being part of this dysfunctional unit. Owen Wilson's philandering author and longtime family friend, Eli Cash, even admits, 'I always wanted to be a Tenenbaum.' (Cash's identity crisis is earlier implied via a magazine profile that refers to him incongruously as 'the James Joyce of the West,' though Anderson has said the character was inspired more by Cormac McCarthy.)

Towards the end of *Tokyo Story*, Shukichi concedes that times have changed, having failed to meaningfully reconnect with Koichi or Shige. He takes his children's professional success and personal security as consolation for their rejection of his traditional values. However, during their stay, Shukichi and Tomi form a close bond with Noriko (Setsuko Hara), the widow of their second son, Shoji, who was killed in the Second World War. Unlike Chas Tenenbaum, who is himself in mourning and is initially distrusting of Royal, Noriko shows nothing but respect to her elders. It is her devotion both to her in-laws and her late husband that ultimately restores Shukichi's faith in the younger generation.

Ironically, Royal's eventual redemption results from his failed attempt to reclaim his seat at the head of the Tenenbaum table. By the time his phoney prognosis is exposed by his supposed romantic rival, Henry Sherman (Danny Glover), he has already succeeded in bringing the whole family together. This consequently allows Chas, Margot, Richie and Eli to overcome their personal struggles and settle their long-standing disputes. It is also significant that *Tokyo Story* and *The Royal Tenenbaums* both feature funeral scenes – nothing inspires reconciliation quite like a death in the family.

Although Ozu's style is distinguished from Anderson's by its stillness and minimalism, both filmmakers are strikingly consistent and precise in their composition, frequently employing symmetrical framing and static interior shots. Ozu's signature 'tatami shot', where the camera is placed in a low, fixed position so that it matches the eyeline of the kneeling actors, is replicated in *The Royal Tenenbaums* during the scene where Margot takes a bath, as well as when she and Richie sit side by side on a couch as Royal expresses his desire to set things right. It also appears later when Margot and Richie confess their love for each other in Richie's tent following his suicide attempt (a scene inspired by Jean-Pierre Melville's 1950 film *Les enfants terribles/ The Strange Ones*). In *The Darjeeling Limited*, Anderson uses a tatami shot when Francis, Jack and Peter have breakfast together, with all three either kneeling or sitting on cushions on the floor, putting them on an equal footing.

Perhaps the most telling comparison between Ozu and Anderson is the cyclical structure of their films. *Tokyo Story* begins and ends with shots of a passing ship and Shukichi sitting quietly at home, first with Tomi as they pack for their trip, and finally as he quietly contemplates his lone existence as a widower. *The Darjeeling Limited* opens and closes with characters running to catch a train. At the start of *The Grand Budapest Hotel* (2014), an unnamed girl is shown clutching a book bearing the name of the film we are about to watch; some 90 minutes later, Anderson returns to the same character reading to herself on a cemetery bench. The very first shot in *The Royal Tenenbaums* is of a same-titled book being checked out of a library, a story-within-a-story framing device Anderson has favoured throughout his career, to be discussed in Chapter 8. However, the prologue sequence opens with a flag emblazoned with the initial 'T' flying proudly atop the Tenenbaum mansion, while the epilogue concludes with a cemetery gate engraved with the family name being closed shut.

In each case, we get the sense not only of a story ending but also of a new one beginning. Royal's death at the end of *The Royal Tenenbaums*, described in typically pithy fashion by Alec Baldwin's narrator, serves a similar function. The jump cut from Royal riding a garbage truck with his grandkids – a shot recycled from earlier in the film, this time with added Chas for an even more joyful experience – to the back of an ambulance creates a disarmingly poignant moment that is straight out of the Ozu playbook. Like the Japanese director's famous cutaway to a boat gently chugging along as it leaves the bay, it leaves us to reflect on the passage of time and the impermanence of life.

FAR LEFT: The official Japanese theatrical poster for *Tokyo Story*.

LEFT: The cast of *Tokyo Story* posing for a publicity still.

OPPOSITE: Ozu invented the so-called 'tatami shot', seen throughout *Tokyo Story* (top) and emulated by Anderson in *The Darjeeling Limited* (bottom) to convey a moment of calm amid the near-constant chaos of the film.

THE CHARLIE BROWN CONNECTION

Anderson's affection for Charles M. Schulz's long-running comic strip, *Peanuts*, and director Bill Melendez's numerous animated adaptations, is no secret. Most of his films contain subtle references to Charlie Brown and the gang. *Rushmore*, for example, shares similarities in characters, with Anderson envisioning Max (Jason Schwarzman) as a cross between Charlie and Snoopy, and his father, like Schulz's, as a barber. There's also Max's winter coat and hat, and certain props, such as the kite he flies and the potted plant he carries. Elsewhere, *Moonrise Kingdom* features a canine character named Snoopy and a sartorial tribute in the form of Suzy's (Kara Hayward) pink dress, modelled after one worn by the Little Red-Haired Girl.

Snoopy's Beagle Scouts are also a clear influence on *Moonrise Kingdom*, and possibly explain the dog Buckley's breed in *The Royal Tenenbaums*. In the same film, the melancholy standard 'Christmas Time is Here', from the Vince Guaraldi Trio's jazz soundtrack to *A Charlie Brown Christmas* (1965), is heard twice: first when Margot leaves her husband Raleigh (Bill Murray) to move back home, and later when she meets her father for lunch. The opening track is a reworking of the traditional German Christmas song 'O Tannenbaum' ('O Christmas Tree'), while the English carol 'Hark! The Herald Angels Sing', covered on the same album, appears in *Rushmore*.

OPPOSITE: *Peanuts* creator Charles M. Schulz at his drawing desk (left). A still from *It's Your First Kiss, Charlie Brown* (right).

ABOVE: Suzy's pink dress in *Moonrise Kingdom* (top) was based on the one worn by Charlie Brown's unrequited sweetheart,

the Little Red-Haired Girl. The zig-zag patterned carpet in Richie Tenenbaum's bedroom (bottom) calls to mind Charlie Brown's jumper.

RIGHT: The LP cover of the *A Charlie Brown Christmas* soundtrack by the Vince Guaraldi Trio.

'LIKE I'VE BEEN TELLING MY WIFE FOR YEARS.
ASIDE FROM SEX – AND SHE'S VERY GOOD AT IT – GODDAMNIT;
I LIKE YOU GUYS BETTER.' – HARRY

OPPOSITE: Blood brothers: The tight yet volatile bond between Archie, Gus and Harry (top) was the primary inspiration for Francis, Jack and Peter Whitman in *The Darjeeling Limited* (bottom).

PART 4
Husbands

(John Cassavetes, 1970)

In a 2010 interview with film critic Richard Brody in the *New Yorker*, Anderson disclosed that, along with Satyajit Ray and Jean Renoir, John Cassavetes had the greatest impact on *The Darjeeling Limited*. 'You know, *Husbands*, there's the three guys, dressed in their suits, and at a certain point, they say, "Let's go to England." And they're all in the moment – they're all on the cusp of some kind of meltdown, and trying to figure out how they're going to continue in their lives, and, you know, Jason and Roman and I watched *Husbands* together, and we really felt connected to it.'

Before that fateful trip to England, *Husbands* starts with a splash. A photo montage introduces four middle-aged male friends at a pool party, mugging and flexing their muscles for the camera like a group of suburban bodybuilders. No sooner has this light-hearted establishing sequence begun, however, than the film cuts to a funeral. Our quartet is already reduced to three. Inspired by the death of the director's older brother Nicholas at the age of 30, *Husbands* tells the story of Archie (Peter Falk), Harry (Ben Gazzara) and Gus (Cassavetes) who, following the sudden death of their close friend Stuart (David Rowlands), career headfirst into an extremely messy midlife crisis.

This boisterous, outwardly macho trio are different in many ways from *The Darjeeling Limited*'s Francis, Peter and Jack, but they share a strong fraternal bond, and there are key similarities in their personalities and interactions, as well as their attire. For example, Harry and Francis are

controlling and impulsive, Gus and Peter are volatile and supercilious, and Archie and Jack are insecure and sensitive. They are depressive, self-destructive and always smartly dressed, save for a brief scene in *Husbands* where the guys play basketball. And despite their constant bickering, both sets of characters are fiercely loyal and dependent on one another – more than they care to admit.

Husbands is described on its poster and in an on-screen title card as 'a comedy about life, death and freedom', a description that could be equally applied to *The Darjeeling Limited*. That said, both films derive discomfort from their humour instead of generating belly laughs. In the case of *Husbands*, the abusive behaviour displayed by the main characters, especially towards women, belies the fact that they are seeking freedom from themselves more than anything else. When Harry flies to London after getting into a violent altercation with his wife, Archie and Gus tag along in an effort to protect their friend from himself.

Similarly, Anderson uses the long journey depicted in *The Darjeeling Limited* to interrogate adult male relationships. Despite all the Whitman brothers' talk of being completely open with each other and to the experience of being in a foreign land, they are not always honest, and their observations about India are quite often facile. 'I love the way this country smells,' Peter says at one point. 'I'll never forget it. It's kind of spicy.' They may agree to 'seek the unknown' and 'say yes to everything', per Francis's request, but they barely modulate their behaviour to allow them to do so in a meaningful or fulfilling way.

Anderson has faced criticism for representing India through a Western lens; for perpetuating lazy stereotypes and failing to properly engage with its culture and customs. But this is precisely the point of *The Darjeeling Limited*. For much of the film, the Whitmans are perfectly content to have their preconceived notions of the country and its people confirmed via Francis's meticulous travel itinerary, which appears to have been cribbed from the CliffsNotes of E.M. Forster's *A Passage to India*. As conspicuous American tourists, they are treated accordingly, and consequently we, the audience, experience India as they do – in a purely superficial way.

It is neither accidental nor an oversight on Anderson's part that the film's setting is portrayed as an extension of the brothers' dynamic: chaotic, noisy, irrational and underdeveloped. When their train becomes lost ('How can a train be lost? It's on rails'), they ignore the obvious sign that it might be time for them to change course. Instead, they latch onto an idle comment made by Francis's assistant, Brendan (Wallace Wolodarsky), 'We haven't located us yet,' interpreting it as a profound piece of wisdom. However, as mentioned earlier in this chapter, it's not until the Whitmans share in someone else's misfortune that they truly begin to find themselves, not to mention the real India.

In *Husbands*, spiritual fulfilment is not on the agenda, but the spontaneous excursion that takes up most of the second half of the film is equally eventful. Taking all their grief and grievances with them across the Atlantic, Archie, Harry and Gus arrive in rain-lashed London and immediately pick up where they left off. They dress up, hit a casino and proceed to gamble (badly), flirt (awkwardly) and drink (heavily). Pretty quickly, it becomes clear that the party is over. The friends are just as riddled with fear and self-loathing as they were before they left New York, and they have no one to blame but themselves.

The Darjeeling Limited concludes with Francis, Jack and Peter finally making peace with their father's passing and symbolically casting off their baggage as they board a different train named the Bengal Lancer, ready for the next stage of their journey. In *Husbands*, Harry decides to stay in England while Archie and Gus return home to their wives and kids. As they step out of the cab they shared from the airport, both men are seen clutching paper bags filled to the brim with stuffed animals and other cheap tokens of repentance.

THE DARJEELING LIMITED'S SETTING IS PORTRAYED AS AN EXTENSION OF THE BROTHERS' DYNAMIC: CHAOTIC, NOISY, IRRATIONAL AND UNDERDEVELOPED

OPPOSITE: The official US theatrical poster for *Husbands* (left), and John Cassavetes directing the action on the set of the film (right).

ABOVE: Archie, Gus and Harry strike a sombre mood following the death of their close friend Stuart (top), which the Whitman brothers mirror on the day of their father's funeral (bottom).

CHAPTER 4

UNDER AUTHORITY

'FOR ME, IT'S SIMPLE. A GOLF COURSE IS FOR GOLF. A TENNIS COURT IS FOR TENNIS. A PRISON CAMP IS FOR ESCAPING.' – CAPITAINE DE BOËLDIEU

OPPOSITE: Fighting
fascism: A group of POWs
give a rousing rendition
of 'La Marseillaise' (top),
a scene Anderson
seemingly tips his hat to
when the staff of the Grand
Budapest await the arrival
of an SS-like organisation
called the 'ZZ' (bottom).

PART 1
La grande illusion

(The Grand Illusion, Jean Renoir, 1937)

Jean Renoir's *La grande illusion* (*The Grand Illusion*) is one of the greatest anti-war films ever made, warning against the evils of tyranny and military aggression with hardly a bullet being fired. The first foreign-language film to be nominated for a Best Picture Oscar, it centres on a band of prisoners of war who find solidarity in their shared struggles, transcending the lines of class and nationality they were previously divided along. It is a quietly profound tale of courage and camaraderie that takes aim at the self-preserving aristocracy while contemplating the collapse of Europe's old order.

After being shot down over enemy territory by a German flying ace named Rittmeister von Rauffenstein (played by the notorious silent-era director Erich von Stroheim, ironically a military deserter), the blue-blooded Capitaine de Boëldieu (Pierre Fresnay) and working-class Lieutenant Maréchal (Jean Gabin) are swiftly captured. However, upon learning of the captain's lofty social status, von Rauffenstein invites the pair to lunch, Renoir already hinting at the 'grand illusion' that such civility should be reserved for the ruling elite.

The Grand Budapest Hotel (2014) strikes a similarly pacifist tone. As the third layer of the film's Russian nesting doll structure is revealed, Jude Law's inquisitive Young Writer recalls that the eponymous hotel had already begun its 'descent into shabbiness and eventual demolition' by the time he first set foot in its vast, once majestic lobby. With this line, Anderson surreptitiously prepares us for a sobering look

at life during wartime in a continent that is teetering, much like the Grand Budapest itself, on the brink of physical and spiritual ruin. Neither Anderson nor Renoir shy away from the harsh realities of war, but at the same time, both are quick to point out the absurdity and futility of it all.

They also show how the smallest gesture of goodwill can improve even the direst situation. The scene in *The Grand Budapest Hotel* where M. Gustave (Ralph Fiennes) and Zero (Tony Revolori) are accosted on a train is testament to this and reminiscent of *La grande illusion*. At first, they have no choice but to acquiesce to the soldiers' strong-arm tactics. But karma intervenes when the affable commanding officer, Henckels (Edward Norton), recognizes M. Gustave as the man who showed him kindness when he was just 'a lonely little boy' (there's a veiled suggestion that M. Gustave may also have been involved with Henckels' mother). These men might be on opposing sides, but they are still able to find common ground.

Although he is not always recognized as such, Anderson is a humanist filmmaker first and foremost. While his characters may display misanthropic tendencies at times, his work is full of empathy and compassion, lightness and warmth. In this regard, he and Renoir are somewhat analogous. As Martin Scorsese noted in a 2008 editorial for the *Criterion Collection*, 'I remember seeing Renoir's films as a child and immediately feeling connected to the characters through his love for them. It's the same with Anderson.'

Just like de Boëldieu and Maréchal, our hero soon finds himself behind bars. After being accused of murdering his octogenarian lover, Madame D. (Tilda Swinton), by her malicious, money-grubbing son Dmitri (Adrien Brody), M. Gustave is sent to a nearby internment camp called Checkpoint 19 (his assigned prisoner number is 112, which is also the emergency telephone number for most of Europe). He wastes no time acquainting himself with the other inmates, including Harvey Keitel's Ludwig, whose crude tattoos are almost identical to those worn by Michel Simon in Jean Vigo's 1934 film *L'Atalante*. Together, they hatch a plan to escape, but it won't be easy: 'Checkpoint 19 ain't no two-bit hoosegow,' as Ludwig puts it. Incidentally, another great film about POWs orchestrating an escape from a prison camp, Billy Wilder's *Stalag 17* (1953), is referenced in *Hotel Chevalier* (2007), Anderson's short prologue to *The Darjeeling Limited* (2007).

Renoir's protagonists attempt to dig their way out, only to be transferred to a different site before they can finish the tunnel. There they are reunited with a fellow prisoner named Rosenthal (Marcel Dalio), a French Jewish banker, and with von Rauffenstein, now serving as the commandant of this heavily guarded fortress. Von Rauffenstein tells them unequivocally that any attempt to escape will be futile, but they set about making a new plan anyway. Meanwhile, in *The Grand Budapest Hotel*, M. Gustave and his convict companions devise an exit strategy as elaborate and intricately layered as a Mendl's cake.

In each case, one man sacrifices himself to give the rest a fighting chance. At first, de Boëldieu uses his privilege to curry favour with von Rauffenstein, but eventually he shows his true colours by providing a distraction for Maréchal and Rosenthal to make a break for it. The underlying sentiment here is that cooperation based on principle, not rank or reputation, is the surest path to progress. Anderson reworks this idea in the form of the Society of the Crossed Keys, a secret fraternity of concierges that rallies behind M. Gustave and Zero.

Although *La grande illusion* depicts the First World War, the timing of its release intimidated the Nazis so much that Joseph Goebbels, the Party's Minister of Propaganda, labelled it 'cinematographic public enemy number one' and ordered every existing print to be destroyed. Fortunately, a German officer and film archivist named Frank Hensel saved the original nitrate negative and had it shipped to Berlin for safekeeping, where it was eventually rediscovered and restored. The film stands today as a monument to the common man and the power of collectivism in times of crisis.

One of the most poignant images in Renoir's film – of POWs standing shoulder to shoulder defiantly singing 'La Marseillaise' – is echoed towards the end of *The Grand Budapest Hotel* in a wide shot of a different but no less exquisitely décored lobby. As banners emblazoned with the mark of an occupying regime hang overhead, the hotel staff await the arrival of the villainous, cartoonishly fascist Dmitri (Adrien Brody). Cleaners, desk clerks, lobby boys and Owen Wilson's concierge present a united front; standing tall, elegant and uncowed, just as M. Gustave would have it.

LEFT: A lobby card used to promote *La grande illusion*.

OPPOSITE: The heavily inked le père Jules (Michel Simon) in Jean Vigo's *L'Atalante* (top) directly inspired Ludwig's body art (bottom), including the initials MAV, meaning 'Mort aux Vaches' or 'Death to Cows', a popular anti-police French anarchist slogan.

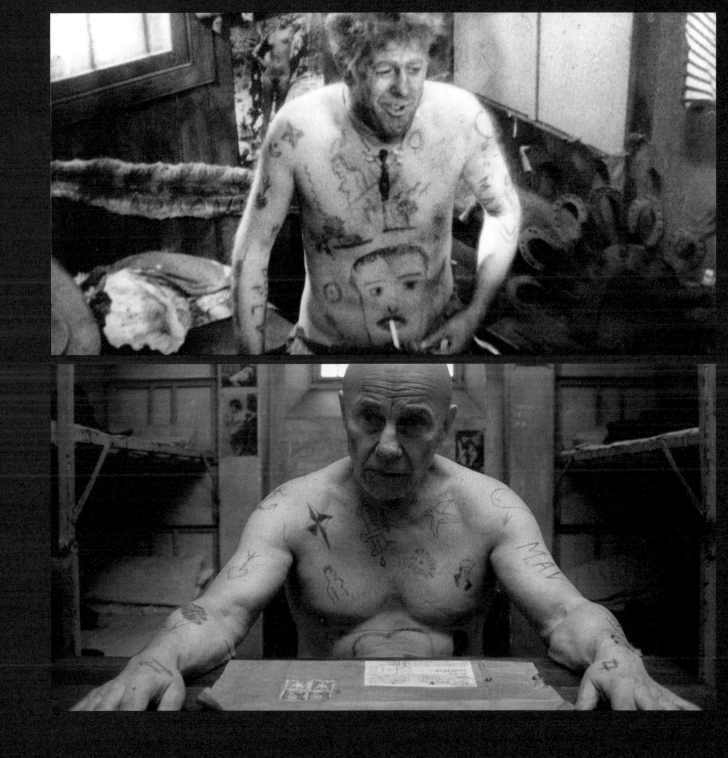

**WHILE ANDERSON'S CHARACTERS
MAY DISPLAY MISANTHROPIC**

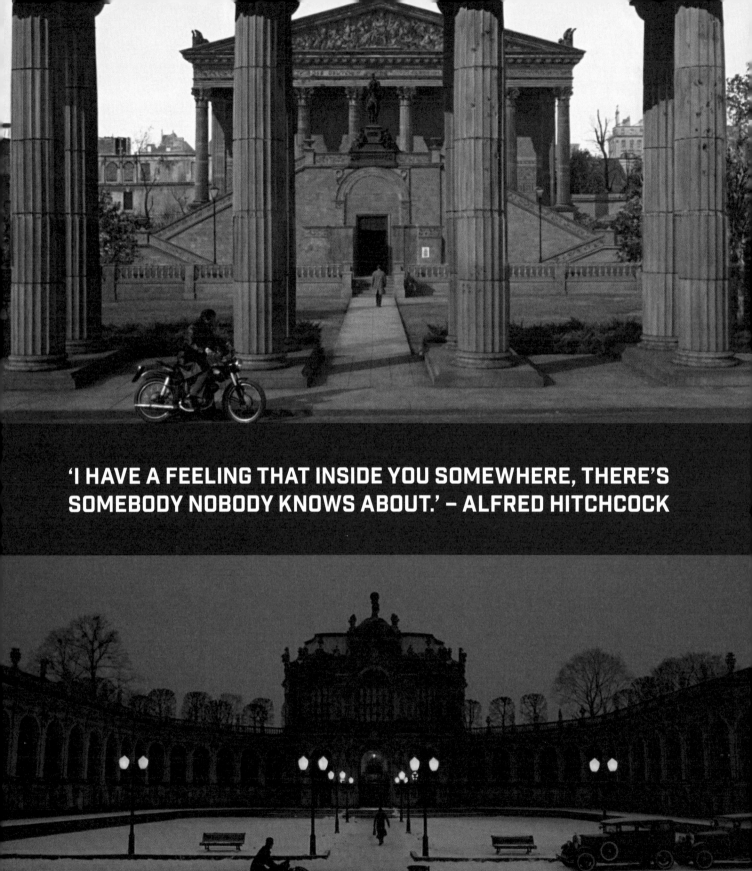

'I HAVE A FEELING THAT INSIDE YOU SOMEWHERE, THERE'S SOMEBODY NOBODY KNOWS ABOUT.' – ALFRED HITCHCOCK

OPPOSITE: Perfect
forgery: Professor
Armstrong is tailed
to Berlin's Alte
Nationalgalerie by a
leather-clad assassin
(top), a scene which
Anderson re-enacts almost
shot-for-shot in *The Grand
Budapest Hotel* when
Kovacs is followed to
the Kunstmuseum by
Jopling (bottom).

PART 2
Torn Curtain

(Alfred Hitchcock, 1966)

While Anderson wears his influences on his sleeve, he tends to do so discreetly. Typically, he pays tribute through subtle clues hidden in characters and costumes, place names and plot details. *The Grand Budapest Hotel* contains a curious exception. The scene where Jeff Goldblum's Deputy Kovacs (named after legendary Hungarian-American cinematographer László Kovács) is stalked by Willem Dafoe's brass-knuckled enforcer, Jopling, is virtually a shot-for-shot re-enactment of a pivotal sequence in Alfred Hitchcock's *Torn Curtain*, from the location, to the way the characters are dressed, to the framing and editing techniques used.

In a conversation with French director Arnaud Desplechin for *Interview Magazine* in 2009, Anderson said:

I think the first director I was ever aware of was Alfred Hitchcock – before I even understood the idea of a director. I was aware of Hitchcock because of *The Alfred Hitchcock Collection*. That was the first time I was aware that there's a guy who is not in the movie who's on the front of the box. He's *responsible*.

Even so, why would Anderson be so blatant in tipping his hat to Hitch? Was it simply his way of acknowledging that no one knew how to stage a chase quite like the Master of Suspense? Perhaps this faithful pastiche conceals a deeper meaning.

Torn Curtain follows Professor Michael Armstrong (Paul Newman), an eminent American physicist who travels to Europe for a conference before announcing, to everyone's shock, that he is defecting to East Germany. His actual plan is to infiltrate the Soviet Union's atomic weapons programme and find the missing piece of a formula that would give the US the upper hand in the Cold War arms race. It's a taut espionage thriller that deftly eschews the hysteria that characterized America's anti-communist crusade during the mid-twentieth century while tapping into the very real contemporary public anxieties about the threat of nuclear annihilation.

The fictional Eastern European republic where *The Grand Budapest Hotel*'s story unfolds is also bracing for war. Accordingly, the Cold War tensions of *Torn Curtain* feel like a useful reference point for Anderson. Yet this alone does not explain Anderson's decision to copy Hitchcock to such a conspicuous and precise degree. (On a related but separate note, during an on-stage Q&A with *New York Times* columnist David Carr in 2014, Anderson jokingly pitched his idea for a James Bond movie: 'I had this one I wanted to do called *Mission Deferred*. My idea was . . . the Cold War is over and there's no gig. [Bond] goes in to see M and M is on the phone, and he's walking around M's office, and finally he says [Anderson, as 007, gestures for M to call him at a more convenient time].')

In preparation for *The Grand Budapest Hotel,* Anderson provided the cast and crew with a viewing list of films of architectural significance, including *Torn Curtain.* When we think of Hitchcock's most iconic films, some of the first images that come to mind are of buildings: the apartment block in *Rear Window* (1954); the bell tower in *Vertigo* (1958); the house behind the Bates motel in *Psycho* (1960); the elementary school in *The Birds* (1963), the list goes on. The same can be said for Anderson: there's Hinckley Cold Storage in *Bottle Rocket* (1996); Rushmore Academy in *Rushmore* (1998); the Tenenbaum mansion in *The Royal Tenenbaums* (2001); the magazine office in *The French Dispatch* (2021); and, of course, the Grand Budapest itself.

Hitchcock was a genius at realizing the dramatic potential of buildings. He had a knack for turning mundane structural features like stairs and windows into grand stages, designing his sets to reflect the emotional or psychological state of the film's protagonist. Anderson, too, often treats architecture as an extension of the conditions, identities and interpersonal relationships of his characters. Given Kovacs' role in determining the legitimacy of various claims to the priceless painting *Boy with Apple,* it is fitting that his ties to the Desgoffe und Taxis estate are (literally) severed in a museum.

In both *Torn Curtain* and *The Grand Budapest Hotel,* the suspense builds as Armstrong and Kovacs, each smartly dressed in a shirt and tie and grey wool overcoat, are trailed across town by trench coat-clad thugs on motorbikes. Eventually, Armstrong arrives at the Alte Nationalgalerie in East Berlin and proceeds calmly but purposefully down the path leading to the front entrance. Once inside, Armstrong quickens his pace, searching for a way out of the eerily quiet museum. Kovacs matches him step for step – as do their respective pursuers. As a side note, while the fictional Kunstmuseum in Anderson's film may resemble the Alte Nationalgalerie, the scene's exterior shots were actually filmed on location at the Zwinger in Dresden, a palatial Baroque-era complex that was all but destroyed during the Second World War and subsequently reconstructed to its original specification, making it a good fit for a film about a great building with a turbulent history.

It could be that there is a metatextual element to *The Grand Budapest Hotel*'s cat-and-mouse museum scene. After all, *Torn Curtain* is a film about the art of the steal;

in this context, Anderson's brazen act of cinematic theft seems to be the perfect crime. However, at the crucial moment when Kovacs appears to have given Jopling the slip, Anderson subverts our expectations of how the scene will end. Instead of mimicking Armstrong by exiting the museum through a rear fire escape door and speeding away in a cab, Kovacs' fate is sealed – or rather, slammed shut – just as freedom beckons.

Apart from switching up the ending, it's worth noting that Anderson injects plenty of his personality into this scene, such as when Kovacs collects a plastic bag containing his deceased cat (Anderson rarely misses an opportunity to skewer a suspenseful moment with morbid humour). Other signature directorial flourishes that distinguish Anderson's version from Hitchcock's include symmetrical composition and incrementally quicker cuts used to reflect Kovacs' heightened sense of urgency. This may be forgery masquerading as homage, but these key differences ensure that Anderson, like Newman's fleet-footed professor, gets away with it.

LEFT: The official US theatrical poster for *Torn Curtain.*

OPPOSITE: Shot-for-shot similarities between the chase scenes for Professor Armstrong (left) and Kovacs (right), although the two men suffer very different fates.

The infamous Bates House that sits behind the motel in *Psycho* (bottom right) is arguably the most iconic building in Alfred Hitchcock's filmography.

**HITCHCOCK
WAS A GENIUS
AT REALIZING
THE DRAMATIC
POTENTIAL
OF BUILDINGS**

POSTCARDS FROM THE PAST

When it came to designing the Grand Budapest, the Library of Congress' Photochrom Print Collection proved an invaluable source of inspiration for Anderson and production designer Adam Stockhausen. They spent weeks poring over the collection, which contains thousands of colourized images of architecture, landscapes, street scenes and daily life across Europe around the turn of the twentieth century, effectively travelling back in time to scout locations that would inform the look and feel of the titular Alpine resort and its surroundings.

In addition, Anderson and Stockhausen borrowed from numerous real-life hotels, such as the Grandhotel Pupp in Karlovy Vary, Czech Republic, the Bristol Palace Hotel in the same city, and the Hotel Börse in Görlitz, Germany, where the main cast stayed throughout principal photography. While the exterior shots of the Grand Budapest were filmed using two hand-built models, a disused department store in Görlitz stood in for the hotel's lobby. Anderson told The Daily Beast in 2014, 'The main reason we ended up in this town was because of this department store that we found. I was trying to find a real hotel but we couldn't.' The Art Nouveau-style department store was opened in 1913 and closed its doors in 2009.

18842. P. Z. · KASSEL · WILHELMSHÖHE, DIE LÖWENBURG

6525. P. Z. · SCHLOSS REINHARDSBRUNN

OPPOSITE: The Grand Budapest in its former glory (far left); the design of the building was inspired by numerous real-life hotels, including the Bristol Palace Hotel (top right) and the Grandhotel Pupp (bottom right) in Karlovy Vary.

ABOVE: Several photocroms from the Library of Congress' vast collection (bottom row) appear on the walls of the Grand Budapest (top and middle), evoking the kind of Mitteleuropean setting that no longer seems to exist.

'HE'S A HANDFUL, BUT HE'S GOT A GOOD HEART.'
– MADAME MINGUET

OPPOSITE: Wild childs:
François sits at the
breakfast table in his latest
foster home (top); fellow
orphan Sam in *Moonrise
Kingdom* (bottom).

PART 3
L'enfance nue

(*Naked Childhood*, Maurice Pialat, 1968)

In the opening moments of *The Grand Budapest Hotel*, the solemn mood is broken by a small act of rebellion as a young boy twice fires a pellet gun at Tom Wilkinson's narrator. (Notice the foreshadowing: the tale we are about to be told will be punctuated by conflict.) Anderson's films often depict children engaging in violence, although it is often harmless and spontaneous rather than premeditated. Indeed, the fact that the boy apologetically re-enters the frame after allowing Wilkinson to finish his monologue betrays how Anderson truly perceives children. Despite their occasional bad behaviour, they are always deserving of compassion and forgiveness.

Maurice Pialat's debut feature *L'enfance nue* (*Naked Childhood*), which Anderson included in a list of his favourite *Criterion Collection* titles in 2010, similarly focuses on youthful transgression. Co-produced by François Truffaut, the film tells the story of François (Michel Terrazon), a ten-year-old orphan whose disobedience and destructiveness result in him being given up by successive foster homes. Although he is perfectly aware of the consequences of, say, stealing a watch, scrapping with his classmates or throwing rail spikes at passing cars, he does so regardless. François craves attention and affection, but his adoptive parents treat him as a nuisance, and deem his behaviour irreconcilable with respectable provincial life.

Unlike François, the Grand Budapest's callow lobby boy, Zero, finds a strong role model in the form of the hotel's avuncular, philandering, liberally perfumed concierge, M. Gustave. Although the pair are more like partners in crime than father and son, they form an instant connection, trading stories, sharing intimate details of their lives and coming to each other's aid on more than one occasion. As their relationship blooms, Zero, a boy without a past, is finally given the chance to write his own story, thanks in part to M. Gustave's tutelage. At the end of the film, Mr Moustafa (F. Murray Abraham, playing an older version of Zero), quotes his mentor, remarking that, 'There are still faint glimmers of civilization left in this barbaric slaughterhouse that was once known as humanity. He was one of them.'

L'enfance nue and *The Grand Budapest Hotel* also share a commonality in the depiction of the shocking death of a pet. In Pialat's film, François, egged on by his peers, drops his sister's cat down a stairwell. In Anderson's film, Deputy Kovacs' grey Persian is tossed out of a window several storeys up by Jopling, a callous act rendered darkly comedic due to the combination of quick editing, the off-camera sound of a decrescendo dying yowl, and Jeff Goldblum's stunned reaction. Both scenes conclude with a God's-eye view shot of said mogs lying splayed on the concrete floor below – miraculously, the cat in *L'enfance nue* survives the initial fall, but François' efforts to nurse it back to health prove to be in vain. While redemption may not be completely beyond him at his tender age, it will not come easily.

Comparing these felicidal incidents is useful because, in nearly every instance where an animal is harmed in one of Anderson's films – and there are many – the perpetrator is an adult. The sole exception is *Moonrise Kingdom* (2012): Camp Ivanhoe's mascot, a wire fox terrier named Snoopy, is killed with an arrow fired by one of the scouts. Crucially, though, the unfortunate pooch was not the intended target. In Anderson's world, the wellbeing of animals is often intrinsically linked to the experiences of young characters, with the mistreatment or death of a pet typically representing the loss of childhood innocence. It's the same in *L'enfance nue*, and also Ken Loach's *Kes* (1969), which has had a similar influence on Anderson and is discussed in Chapter 6. Anderson does not view all children as wholly innocent or pure, nor does he portray them as irredeemable. But they are never shown to be capable of the deliberate cruelty displayed by François.

Consider *Moonrise Kingdom*'s precocious male protagonist, Sam (Jared Gilman). Like François, Sam is an orphan and an outcast who shows a flagrant disregard for authority. He is described as having 'emotional issues' and doesn't seem to fit in with the Khaki Scouts or in wider society – it's telling that one of the patches embroidered onto his uniform says '3rd Class'. And like François, who is eventually taken in by the more attentive Minguets, played by a real-life foster couple whose personal story Pialat based the characters on, Sam eventually receives protection from someone who recognizes his inherent qualities; someone not all that different from him.

It's easy to see why Sam and Bruce Willis' mild-mannered Captain Sharp get along so well. Both are lonely, misunderstood souls whose introverted nature masks a maverick streak. At one point, Edward Norton's Scout Master Ward describes Sam as the camp's 'least popular scout . . . by a significant margin'. And while Captain Sharp may be little more than a 'sad, dumb policeman', according to Sam's girlfriend Suzy (Kara Hayward), there's a heart of gold behind that pristinely polished badge. Simply put, Sam and Captain Sharp were made for each other.

L'enfance nue and *Moonrise Kingdom* are told from the perspectives of misguided delinquents who are given a second chance. They each capture familiar childhood feelings: fear of abandonment; yearning for (mis)adventure; uncertainty about the future; alienation, exuberance and inadequacy. Yet these films have starkly contrasting outcomes. While François is taken away from the Minguets and sent to a young offenders' institute – the 'nakedness' of the title unambiguously laid bare – Sam remains in the care of Captain Sharp. One boy has his hopes and freedoms stripped away by the state, the other is rescued by it in a different sense.

L'ENFANCE NUE AND MOONRISE KINGDOM EACH CAPTURE FAMILIAR CHILDHOOD FEELINGS: FEAR OF ABANDONMENT; YEARNING FOR (MIS)ADVENTURE; UNCERTAINTY ABOUT THE FUTURE; ALIENATION, EXUBERANCE AND INADEQUACY

ABOVE: The young François' mistreatment of a cat (left) is mirrored by Jopling (right); both ending in God's-eye view shots of the felicidal event.

RIGHT: Director Maurice Pialat (left) and the French theatrical poster for L'enfance nue (right).

une réalisation de MAURICE PIALAT

L'ENFANCE NUE

MICHEL TARRAZON
LINDA GUTENBERG
RAOUL BILLEREY
PIERRETTE DEPLANQUE

CLAUDE BERRI

MAURICE PIALAT

Le premier film de Maurice Pialat : un coup de Maître !
en copies neuves à partir du 24 février 2010

'THE REVOLUTION'S NO PARTY. IT'S NOT MADE
LIKE A WORK OF ART.' – VERONIQUE

OPPOSITE: Best face forward: Jean-Luc Godard's use of fourth-wall-breaking close-up is present throughout *La chinoise*, from Véronique's salute to Guillaume's smoky stare (top). In *The French Dispatch*, Anderson frames Lucinda and Juliette in the same way (bottom), even copying Godard's colour palette.

PART 4
La chinoise

(*The Chinese*, Jean-Luc Godard, 1967)

Characters under siege is a recurring theme in Anderson's films. In *Moonrise Kingdom*, Sam and Suzy attempt to shake off Tilda Swinton's Social Services and the other adults atop the church where they first meet. In *Fantastic Mr. Fox* (2009), Mr Fox (voiced by George Clooney) and his furry allies burrow furiously beneath the ground as Boggis (Robin Hurlstone), Bunce (Hugo Guiness) and Bean (Helen McCrory) stage an ambush. In *Isle of Dogs* (2018), Atari (Koyu Rankin) and his newfound canine companions defend their trashtopia from a robot onslaught. And in *The French Dispatch*, Timothée Chalamet's overzealous undergraduate Zeffirelli organizes a non-violent revolt against the conservative establishment of Ennui-sur-Blasé.

'Revisions to a Manifesto', the second of three stories in Anderson's paean to print journalism, *The French Dispatch*, is presented as a longform magazine article narrated by Frances McDormand's dutiful, cynical and ethically compromised expat reporter, Lucinda Krementz. It chronicles the so-called 'Chessboard Revolution', led by Chalamet's self-styled firebrand, Zeffirelli (named after the Italian film and theatre director Franco Zeffirelli), and was directly inspired by Mavis Gallant's two-part reportage series 'The Events in May: A Paris Notebook' about the student uprising of 1968, published in the *New Yorker* in September of that year.

Beyond its obvious narrative allusions to May 1968, 'Revisions to a Manifesto' draws upon several French New Wave films, namely François Truffaut's *Les quatre cents coups* (*The 400 Blows*, 1959, which you can read more about in Chapter 1), Louis Malle's *Le feu follet* (*The Fire Within*, 1963) and Jean-Luc Godard's *Masculin féminin* (*Masculine Feminine*, 1966), the last evidenced by the appearance of its title on a sign above a hairdresser's storefront. Additionally, the Claude Channes song 'Mao Mao' (1967), featured in Godard's film, is covered by Jarvis Cocker in *The French Dispatch*. Chief among these influences is Godard's agitprop farce *La chinoise* (*The Chinese*), which foreshadowed the radical social and political changes that would sweep through the French capital 12 months later.

The majority of *La chinoise* takes place in a small apartment on Paris's Rue de Miromesnil, which was owned by Godard and his then-wife, Anne Wiazemsky, who portrays Véronique in the film. The story concerns the Aden Arabie Cell, a collective of five middle-class student activists named after a book by the French philosopher Paul Nizan. They spend the film engaging in an ideological dialogue regarding the implications of the Chinese Cultural Revolution, while simultaneously railing against French colonialism, the ongoing Vietnam War and, more broadly, the effects of Western imperialism in Southeast Asia.

La chinoise can also be seen as an exercise in self-satire. One of the pronouncements daubed on the wall of the students' apartment reads '*il faut confronter les idées vagues avec des images claires*' ('it is necessary to confront vague ideas with clear images'). This is by turns a bold declaration of intent and a sly critique of the notion that radical art alone can serve as a valid form of political action. Here, Godard is not skewering the students and their anti-bourgeois proselytizing but rather his own pseudo-revolutionary pretensions.

At the time of its release, *The French Dispatch* drew criticism in some quarters for supposedly trivializing the events of May 1968. However, Anderson seems to be more concerned with the aesthetics of protest rather than the politics themselves. He's interested in the way his characters dress, the language they use and the mass-produced images they consume and create. Anderson's characters are, as Godard might say, 'the children of Marx and Coca-Cola'. Likewise, 'Revisions to a Manifesto' revolves around a self-deprecating joke. Zeffirelli and his spotty, cheroot-smoking cohorts are not campaigning on behalf of any greater cause but for free access to the girls' dormitory. In reality, the initial protests of the students at the Université Paris Nanterre were based on similar demands, although the heavy-handed response by the French authorities sparked a nationwide movement that ultimately escalated into a general strike.

The segment is filled with sight gags designed to underscore the fact that Zeffirelli is neither a prodigious wordsmith nor a true socialist, but merely a horny teenage agitator. For example, the image of him writing his manifesto in the bath with a towel wrapped around his head evokes Jacques-Louis David's famous painting, *The Death of Marat*, which depicts the artist's assassinated friend Jean-Paul Marat, a key figure in the French Revolution. Above Zeffirelli's bed sits a photograph of the Nobel Prize-winning novelist and poet Boris Pasternak, who was considered one of the brightest minds of Russia's post-revolutionary period. And in the café where Zeffirelli and his comrades meet to drink, dance and debate, there is a poster advertising a fictional brand of absinthe called 'Les Aveugles', literally 'The Blind', a reference to both the spirit's supposed adverse side effects and a poem of the same name by Charles Baudelaire, who is credited with coining the French term *flâneur*, meaning 'stroller' or 'loafer'.

LEFT: A poster seen in *La chinoise* (top) echoing the posters of the May 1968 demonstrations, such as this one produced by the Atelier Populaire des Beaux-Arts, France (bottom).

OPPOSITE: Zeffirelli revising his manifesto in a bathtub, towel wrapped around his head (top), is reminiscent of Jacques-Louis David's 1793 painting *The Death of Marat* (bottom left), himself a famous French revolutionary leader.

A photo of the Russian poet and novelist Boris Pasternak in the Urals in 1916 (bottom right) appears on the wall above Zeffirelli's bed (middle right).

ZEFFIRELLI IS NEITHER A PRODIGIOUS WORDSMITH NOR A TRUE SOCIALIST, BUT MERELY A HORNY TEENAGE AGITATOR

Anderson cribs from *La chinoise* in other ways. Lyna Khoudri, who plays Juliette, is styled to resemble a cross between Wiazemsky and another of Godard's muses, Anna Karina; also, her white moped helmet is similar to the one Pascale Ogier wears in Jacques Rivette's *Le pont du Nord* (1981). The radio tower from which Zeffirelli fatefully broadcasts his revised manifesto is a nod to the pirate station 'Radio Peking', which incessantly blares out news bulletins and Maoist dictums. Actors are frequently framed in symmetrical close-up, an Anderson trademark that he inherited in part from Godard. And the red-and-blue colour coding that Godard masterfully employs in films such as *La chinoise* and *Pierrot le fou* (*Pierrot the Fool*, 1965) is replicated in the aforementioned radio-tower scene,

as well as the slow motion shot of Juliette and Zeffirelli riding a Mobylette in reverie.

'Revisions to a Manifesto' opens with Zeffirelli, soon-to-be-martyred poster boy of Ennui's 'pimple cream and wet dream contingent', locked in a board game battle with a university professor, and closes with a school bell and an empty swing set, signalling a return to normality. *La chinoise* concludes with the members of Aden Arabie being forced to vacate the apartment when its owners return from their summer holiday. With the group having been unsuccessful in their efforts, Véronique concedes that she has only taken 'the first timid steps on a long march' and contemplates her return to school.

TOP: Blue and red feature heavily in Godard's film, from Véronique's shirt (left) to the curtains and books that frame Yvonne (right).

BOTTOM: Anderson uses these same colours during Zeffirelli's electrocution (left) and the dream-like sequence where he and Juliette ride a moped together (right).

OPPOSITE: The American writer and civil rights activist James Baldwin (top left) was the inspiration for Roebuck Wright (top right), while J.K.L. Berensen (bottom right) was based on the American journalist and art historian Rosamond Bernier (bottom left).

NEW YORKER, I LOVE YOU

Many of the characters in *The French Dispatch* are based on real people, and several are associated with the *New Yorker*, which Anderson has been an avid reader of since grade school. Bill Murray's terse but rigorous editor, Arthur Howitzer, Jr., is an amalgamation of the *New Yorker's* first two editors, Harold Ross and William Shawn; Ross founded the magazine in 1925, the same year that *The French Dispatch* was founded. Jeffrey Wright's fastidious food critic, Roebuck Wright, is a proxy for James Baldwin (with, per Wright's own description, a dash of A.J. Liebling and Tennessee Williams for good measure). Adrien Brody's highly strung art dealer/tax dodger, Julian Cadazio, was inspired by the British art dealer Sir Joseph Duveen, who was the subject of a 1951 *New Yorker* profile. Tilda Swinton's oversharing art pundit, J.K.L. Berensen, is a near-perfect forgery of the art writer and lecturer Rosamond Bernier. Then there's Lucinda Krementz, who shares a name with the famed *New Yorker* photographer and author Jill Krementz, the author of some 30 books and spouse of the writer Kurt Vonnegut for as many years. In addition to Krementz, Anderson modelled the character on Lillian Ross, who worked as a staff writer at the *New Yorker* for more than seven decades, and whose private collection of the long-running periodical Anderson is currently the caretaker of. Anderson has also admitted there is something of Frances McDormand in Lucinda, telling the magazine in 2021, 'I once heard her say to a very snooty French waiter, "Kindly leave me my dignity."'

CHAPTER 5

GREAT ESCAPES

'IT WAS BETTER TO LIVE A WEEK WITH SOMEONE WHO LOVED ME FOR WHAT I WAS, THEN YEARS OF LONELINESS.' – HOLLY

OPPOSITE: Rebels with a cause: Kit rests on his trusty Savage 99R rifle (top), looking like James Dean, as Holly tells him. The character was one of the chief inspirations for Sam in *Moonrise Kingdom*, who copies many of Kit's gestures and mannerisms (bottom).

BELOW: The original US LP pressing of Bruce Springsteen's 1982 studio album *Nebraska*.

PART 1
Badlands

(Terrence Malick, 1973)

Despite a boilerplate disclaimer stating that *Badlands* does not intend 'to depict real events or persons, living or dead', the film was loosely inspired by the real-life story of serial killer Charles Starkweather and his girlfriend-turned-accomplice Caril Ann Fugate, who embarked on a week-long rampage in January 1958 that resulted in the murders of ten people, adding to the life Starkweather took in late 1957. Their crimes have inspired several films, including Tony Scott's *True Romance* (1993), a spiritual remake of *Badlands*, and Oliver Stone's *Natural Born Killers* (1994), as well as Bruce Springsteen's 1982 song 'Nebraska'.

In Terrence Malick's version of events, Holly (Sissy Spacek), a baton-twirling girl-next-door, meets Kit (Martin Sheen), a James Dean type from the wrong side of the tracks, while he's working as a garbage collector outside her home in smalltown South Dakota. They fall in love and before long find themselves forging a haphazard path across the American Midwest, leaving a trail of bodies in their wake. All the while, Holly records her thoughts in her journal, which we hear snippets of throughout the film via Spacek's lilting voiceover.

Moonrise Kingdom (2012) also uses spoken narration to reveal Sam (Jared Gilman) and Suzy's (Kara Hayward) plan to run away together, which they hatch in secret through a series of letters. The expositional 'Dear Sam; Dear Suzy' sequence affords us an intimate glimpse into the pen pals'

unhappy home lives (a similar device is used in Leonard Kastle's 1970 film *The Honeymoon Killers*). Anderson's lovers on the lam are by no means violent killers, but they do have a few things in common with Kit and Holly, as indicated by the title of a book Suzy finds above the fridge in her parents' kitchen: *Coping with the Very Troubled Child*. Indeed, all four characters could be described as very troubled children.

Sam is nowhere near as trigger-happy as Kit, though he is willing to use his air rifle when the occasion calls for it and, in his correspondence with Suzy, he admits to having started a fire at his foster home despite claiming to have no memory of doing so; his sleepwalking theory is disputed by his foster parents, suggesting that it may not have been an isolated incident. Like Sam, Kit commits arson in *Badlands*, setting Holly's house ablaze after shooting her father (played by Warren Oates) dead and dumping his body in the basement.

As they flee the scene, Kit's confession-cum-faux-suicide-note is played out on a vinyl record, made a few hours earlier on a Voice-O-Graph machine in town.

After meeting at their planned rendezvous point, Sam and Suzy venture into the wilderness to start a new life together with the Khaki Scouts, Captain Sharp (Bruce Willis) and Suzy's parents hot on their tails. Similarly, before reaching the titular 'badlands' of Montana, Kit and Holly take shelter in a forest, where they construct an impressive treehouse and live off the land for a time. We see them fishing, gathering firewood and dancing to popular songs of the era, blissfully unaware of the danger they have put themselves in.

While it appears that Kit is merely feigning military experience, he, like Sam, demonstrates good survival instincts. Meanwhile, Holly dutifully assumes her role as Bonnie to Kit's Clyde. She reads to him from Norwegian writer Thor Heyerdahl's 1948 book *The Kon-Tiki Expedition* – another great adventure story – and paints her eyes with heavy makeup 'to see how they'd come out'. As Matt Zoller Seitz has pointed out, this shot is replicated in *Moonrise Kingdom* when Suzy is backstage getting ready for a recital of Benjamin Britten's opera *Noye's Fludde*, based on the biblical story of Noah and the flood.

These scenes in *Badlands*, which are the most beautiful and tender in the film, are set to a famous piece of music by German composers Carl Orff and Gunild Keetman, most commonly known as 'Gassenhauer' ('Street Song'). The music perfectly encapsulates the childlike spirit of the film's protagonists. Malick licensed a handful of Orff-Keetman compositions from the LP series *Musica Poetica: Orff-Schulwerk*, with 'Bläserstücke Pastourelles' ('Passion') and in particular 'Musik zu einem Puppenspiel' ('Music for a Puppet Play') providing Alexandre Desplat with the creative spark for his original score for Anderson's film. *Badlands* also includes the song 'Mariae Geburt' ('The Birth of the Virgin Mary'), which features a female choir whose dulcet tones are echoed in the children's chorus heard in *Moonrise Kingdom*.

Inevitably, Kit and Holly's stay in their makeshift paradise is short-lived. They are tracked down by a trio of bounty hunters and forced to hit the road again, where the killing continues. It's at this point that doubt starts to creep into Holly's mind. Expressing her disillusionment and

concern over what the future might hold for her and Kit, she muses: 'The world was like a faraway planet to which I could never return. I thought what a fine place it was full of things that people can look into and enjoy.' A similar feeling of uncertainty permeates Sam and Suzy's elopement. After decamping to a secluded beach which they rename in honour of their love, as revealed in the penultimate shot of the film, they are rumbled and forced to return to their separate lives.

In the end, both couples are apprehended. (Curiously, right before Kit is arrested, he builds a ceremonial stack of rocks, just as Jack Whitman, played by Jason Schwarzman, does in *The Darjeeling Limited*, 2007.) In Sam and Suzy's case, however, the punishment is not nearly as severe, and they are not kept apart for long. Neither they nor Kit and Holly express any regret for their actions or the distress they have caused everyone, only the fact that their romantic escapades couldn't go on forever. The Boss summed it up best: 'I can't say that I'm sorry for the things that we done / At least for a little while, sir, me and her we had us some fun.'

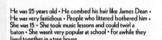

He was 25 years old • He combed his hair like James Dean • He was very fastidious • People who littered bothered him • She was 15 • She took music lessons and could twirl a baton • She wasn't very popular at school • For awhile they lived together in a tree house.

In 1959, she watched while he killed a lot of people.

LEFT: The official US theatrical poster for *Badlands*.

OPPOSITE: Scout Master Ward (top left) bears a striking resemblance to the main subject of *The Scoutmaster*, 1956 by Norman Rockwell (right). Rockwell displaying his work at a boy scout jamboree, c. 1950 (bottom left).

SCOUT'S HONOUR

Much of the visual style of *Moonrise Kingdom* was inspired by another great American artist, as production designer Adam Stockhausen told *Uproxx* in 2012: 'Wes really wanted the Khaki Scouts to have a unique visual style of its own. So we looked at the Norman Rockwell paintings [for the Boy Scouts of America].' Rockwell's long association with the BSA began in 1915 when he became the art editor for *Boys' Life* magazine at the age of 19. Over the course of his career, he created 49 original pieces for the annual Boy Scout calendar (between 1925 and 1976), providing an invaluable resource for Anderson and Stockhausen.

Rockwell's highly nostalgic and patriotic scenes show Scouts engaging in all kinds of thrilling activities and virtuous deeds, but Anderson was specifically interested in the period they represent. *Moonrise Kingdom* is set in 1965, which the director told the *Hollywood Reporter* after the film's Cannes premiere 'is really the end of one kind of America'. There is also a certain likeness between Edward Norton's bumbling troop leader and the comparatively serene subject of Rockwell's 1956 painting *The Scoutmaster*, which was based on multiple photographs taken on the artist's visit to the 1953 National Scout Jamboree in Irvine, California.

OPPOSITE: Just as Kit and Holly try their hands at fishing (top) and building a treehouse in the woods (bottom right), so do Sam and Suzy during their brief abscondment (middle; bottom left).

ABOVE: Several more moments in *Moonrise Kingdom* (left column) that are clear visual references to *Badlands* (right column).

'Y'KNOW, KID . . . YOU GOT A HELLUVA KNACK FOR KILLIN' A CONVERSATION.' – BUDDUSKY

OPPOSITE: Journeymen: The way Buddusky, Mulhall and Meadows are framed at the start of their long and somewhat aimless mission (top) is evoked by Anderson during the Whitman brothers' soul-searching trip aboard the Darjeeling Limited (bottom).

PART 2
The Last Detail

(Hal Ashby, 1973)

Throughout this book, I have chosen to focus on one film per director in order to show the breadth and depth of Anderson's pool of cinematic influences. But in the case of Hal Ashby, it's worth making an exception, not least because of how varied his films are and the multitude of ways they have inspired Anderson.

In the same interview with *GOOD Magazine* cited in Chapter 2, Anderson mentions *The Last Detail* in relation to *The Darjeeling Limited*:

> I watched this movie with my collaborators Roman [Coppola] and Jason [Schwartzman] because we were getting ready to make a movie about three sort of confused boys on a train, and *The Last Detail* follows more or less the same lines . . . it does not have a terrific plot, and maybe it might not have one at all – and that was encouraging to us because we didn't have one either.

(As a side note, in *The Royal Tenenbaums*, 2001, Gene Hackman utters the phrase 'let's shag ass'; the same peculiar expression appears in *The Last Detail*, implying that Ashby's irreverent sense of humour appeals to Anderson as much as his somewhat unconventional approach to narrative filmmaking.)

Based on Darryl Ponicsan's eponymous 1970 novel, Ashby's follow-up to *Harold and Maude* (1971) was made towards the tail-end of the Vietnam War. It chronicles five days in the lives of two jaded navy 'lifers' and the court-martialled seaman they have been tasked with escorting from their headquarters in Norfolk, Virginia, to Portsmouth Naval Prison in Maine. But when Signalman First Class Billy 'Badass' Buddusky (Jack Nicholson) and Gunner's Mate First Class Richard 'Mule' Mulhall (Otis Young) learn that 18-year-old Larry Meadows (Randy Quaid) has been sentenced to eight years in the brig for attempting to steal $40 from a charity collection tin, they decide to give the timid young sailor one last taste of freedom the only way they know how: get him drunk; get him laid; and get him into even more trouble.

The making of *The Last Detail* was a relatively painless experience for Ashby, despite the US Navy refusing him permission to film at their Norfolk base. But a difficult post-production period saw the director fire editor Ken Zemke, replacing him with Robert C. Jones. Meanwhile, executives at Columbia Pictures sweated over the film's excessive use of the F-bomb; the heavily redacted theatrical cut still contained 65 uses of the word – what else would you expect from sailors – which was a record at the time. Still, audiences responded well in early test screenings, and Ashby convinced the studio to submit the film to the Cannes Film Festival, where Nicholson was awarded the Best Actor prize in 1974. Following the critical and commercial failure of *Harold and Maude*, the praise lavished upon *The Last Detail* marked a redemptive moment for Ashby at a crucial juncture in his filmmaking career.

Recalling his first viewing of *The Last Detail* at the University of Texas in 1988, Anderson said, 'I was struck by its stark sadness, and by the desperation of its characters to snap out of the monotony and repression of their gloomy, Eastern, military winter.' The basic human desire to break free from the economic, social and political systems that are designed to curb individual autonomy and self-expression is central to many of Anderson's films, particularly *Bottle Rocket* (1996), *The Royal Tenenbaums* and *The Darjeeling Limited*. In the last, the Whitman brothers trek across India with a general air of apathy that evokes Buddusky, Mulhall and Meadows' fitful journey by road and rail along the Eastern Seaboard. Both sets of men lack direction and seek new experiences, finding them in some unexpected places. Both films also feature misguided attempts to reunite characters with their mothers, who prove elusive in different ways.

In *The Last Detail*, our protagonists make a detour to a bar where they are picked up by four visibly hip young women. One of them asks Mulhall how he feels about having served in Vietnam. He responds with a sigh: 'Man says go, gotta do what the Man says. We're livin' in this Man's world, ain't we?' Mulhall's shrugging acceptance of his role in one of the bloodiest and most unpopular military conflicts in American history reveals where Ashby's – and Ponicsan's – sympathies lie. Although the director cultivated a shaggy-haired hippie persona during the early part of his career, he was more of a maverick than an out-and-out radical. Still, Ashby makes it clear in *The Last Detail* that he is firmly on the sailors' side.

Later in the film, Buddusky, Mulhall and Meadows try and fail to cook hot dogs in a frozen park, a perfect metaphor for the impotence of American imperialism. They sit hunched and shivering on benches facing in opposite directions, still wearing their uniforms, looking completely lost; their service to their country having turned them into social pariahs. Unable to imagine a better life for himself outside of the navy, Buddusky repeatedly expresses his desire to return to sea. Although Meadows is the one facing time, his chaperones both know what it's like to have your liberties curtailed. Recognizing that they are duty bound to complete their shore patrol detail, Buddusky and Mulhall ultimately deliver Meadows to the naval prison. Their subversion of the powers that dictate their lives has amounted to little more than a modest per diem frittered away on partying and prostitutes.

Bottle Rocket, too, is an existential road movie about a band of outsiders who are impulsive and reckless in their attempts to stick it to the Man. But more than that, it's a film about self-discovery and personal growth, about taking control of your destiny by embracing a more authentic and meaningful existence (at least from Anthony's perspective). Despite Dignan's (Owen Wilson) elaborate 75-year plan for him and Anthony (Luke Wilson), which initially involves pulling off numerous heists while ingratiating themselves with a local landscaper/part-time crook, Anderson's debut, like *The Last Detail*, finally arrives at the conclusion that even the most exhilarating joyride will eventually run out of gas.

BELOW: The first edition paperback cover of Darryl Ponicsan's 1970 novel *The Last Detail* (left); and the US theatrical one-sheet poster for the film adaptation (right).

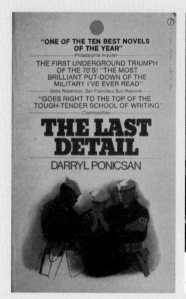

THE PRAISE LAVISHED UPON *THE LAST DETAIL* MARKED A REDEMPTIVE MOMENT FOR ASHBY

ABOVE: Buddusky, Mulhall and Meadows hit a collective low point in a frosty park (top). Earlier, the trio appear more connected as they catch a cross-country bus (middle left), a shot which Anderson repurposes near the end of the Whitman brothers' journey (bottom left).

Jack Nicholson and Otis Young share a light-hearted moment with director Hal Ashby on set (bottom right).

'THE SEA, ONCE IT CASTS ITS SPELL, HOLDS ONE IN ITS NET OF WONDER FOREVER.' – JACQUES-YVES COUSTEAU

OPPOSITE: Close knit:
Jacques-Yves Cousteau
aboard a helicopter (top);
and Steve Zissou, whose
appearance was based on
Cousteau, shortly before
a fateful crash (bottom).

PART 3
Le monde du silence

(*The Silent World*, Jacques-Yves Cousteau, Louis Malle, 1956)

Billed as 'a motion picture studio 165ft under the sea,' Jacques-Yves Cousteau and Louis Malle's *Le monde du silence* (*The Silent World*) represents a (heavily dramatized) milestone in wildlife documentary filmmaking. Shot over a two-year period, the film follows the famed oceanographer on his research vessel *Calypso*, as he and his crew enjoy life on the open waves, occasionally dropping anchor to enter a mysterious underwater realm. This was the full-length directorial debut of both Cousteau and Malle, and it has a chaotic, on-the-fly energy that Anderson channels in *The Life Aquatic with Steve Zissou* (2004).

It's no secret that Anderson modelled the title character of his film, played by Bill Murray with morose relish, on Cousteau. Yet evidence of the French adventurer's influence on Anderson can be found much earlier in his filmography. In *Rushmore* (1998), Max (Jason Schwartzman) checks out a copy of Cousteau and Philippe Diolé's book *Diving for Sunken Treasure* from the school library, which chronicles the *Calypso*'s voyage to the Caribbean to recover the spoils from the wreck of a Spanish galleon. Inside the book, he notices a hand-written quote attributed to Cousteau: 'When one man, for whatever reason, has the opportunity to lead an extraordinary life, he has no right to keep it to himself.' This quote becomes Max's mantra.

Although Max is an avid collector of extracurricular activities, it is revealed early in the film that he is failing academically. Despite this, he has the air of someone who

is destined for greatness, or rather, someone who believes himself destined for greatness. Like Cousteau, he craves excitement and dreams of escaping the monotony of his life on dry land. The discovery of the Cousteau quote leads Max to Miss Cross (Olivia Williams), but this scene also has a symbolic dimension: as these are the words of a world-renowned scuba diver, the subtle implication is that Max, at least when it comes to romantically pursuing a woman twice his age, is out of his depth.

Going further back, in *Bottle Rocket*, Cousteau even makes a brief appearance on screen: a black-and-white portrait of him is shown hanging in Mr Henry's (James Caan) swanky Texas pad. However, *The Life Aquatic with Steve Zissou* is where Anderson's obsession with Cousteau really comes to the surface. Firstly, Zissou's ship, the *Belafonte* (named after the Jamaican-American singer and actor Harry Belafonte, whose hit 1956 debut LP *Calypso* is credited with introducing the eponymous genre to American audiences), closely resembles the *Calypso* and even has a similar backstory. During the boat-tour sequence, Zissou explains that it was once a long-range submarine hunter, and that he acquired it from the US Navy (in reality, both the *Calypso* and the ship that appears in the film were former minesweepers originally commissioned for the Royal Navy). The miniature ship he is holding at the start of this scene is actually a model of the *Calypso* with the hull painted blue. The *Belafonte* is not your average frigate. It's fitted with an editing suite, a mini sub (inspired by Cousteau's 'Diving Saucer'), a helicopter, a sauna, a science lab and a fully stocked kitchen containing 'probably the most technologically advanced equipment on the ship'. Additionally, it boasts a research library with a complete first edition set of *The Life Aquatic with Steve Zissou* companion series, whose covers are identical to the first editions of Cousteau's books, as seen in *Rushmore*. The ship is staffed by a veritable motley crew who are all styled like Zissou, and by extension, Cousteau: bright-red watch caps; light-blue button-down shirts; matching slacks; and navy-blue knitted sweaters.

On top of that, the illustrated posters seen throughout the film are an homage to those used to promote Cousteau's deep-sea odysseys, particularly *Le monde du silence*, *Le monde sans soleil* (*World Without Sun*, 1964) and *Voyage au bout du monde* (*Voyage to the Edge of the World*, 1976). The latter was directed by Cousteau's son Philippe, who died in a seaplane accident aged 38 – the same tragic fate that befalls Zissou's supposed biological son Ned (Owen Wilson). Curiously, a man in a pilot's uniform appears on the top deck of the *Belafonte* during the end credits, which was inspired by *The Adventures of Buckaroo Banzai Across the 8th Dimension* (1984), where all the characters, dead and living, are brought back for a final curtain call.

Anderson's film lifts many details directly from *Le monde du silence*. Zissou's crew also wear yellow aqualungs, which Cousteau co-invented with French engineer Émile Gagnan, as part of their diving gear. Both the Belafonte and the Calypso have observation chambers beneath the bow. Zissou and Cousteau each narrate their films, introducing the individual members of their crews, explaining the scientific nature of their work, and describing the various creatures they encounter with an infectious sense of wonder.

In addition to all this Cousteau minutiae, *The Life Aquatic with Steve Zissou* depicts a menagerie of spectacular make-believe animals, such as crayon ponyfish, sugar crabs, wild snow mongoose, electric jellyfish (wrongly identified), rhinestone bluefin tuna, and, of course, the enigmatic jaguar shark that devoured Zissou's close friend and seafaring partner Esteban du Plantier (Seymour Cassel). The revenge mission that serves as *The Life Aquatic with Steve Zissou*'s dramatic lynchpin has its roots in *Le monde du silence*. When a group of sharks began feasting on the carcass of a young sperm whale that was fatally maimed by the *Calypso*'s propeller, Cousteau's crew retaliated, killing as many as they could.

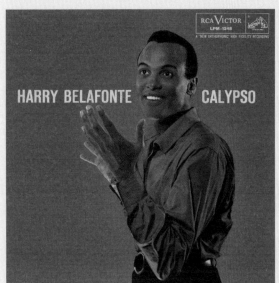

FAR LEFT: Harry Belafonte's 1956 studio album *Calypso*, which inspired both the names of Cousteau's and Zissou's ships.

LEFT: Zissou's yellow submersible (top) was based on a similar vessel once operated by Cousteau's crew. In Rushmore's library, Max discovers a copy of Cousteau and Philippe Diolé's 1978 book *Diving for Sunken Treasure* (bottom).

OPPOSITE: Anderson pays homage to Cousteau and Louis Malle's film (middle and bottom right) with similar shots in *The Life Aquatic with Steve Zissou* (top and bottom left).

Le monde du silence's title has a tragic, unintended double meaning. Throughout the film, along with an innate curiosity with the sea, Cousteau displays a surprisingly cavalier attitude towards the things living in it. He and his crew are filmed hacking away huge chunks of coral reef and even using dynamite to take a census of the marine life in one area. 'For every ten fish killed,' Cousteau says with casual indifference, 'only one or two float to the surface: the rest sink.' Although Cousteau makes every effort to present himself as a heroic figure, he was evidently more of a colonizer than a conservationist at this time.

Zissou is no less flawed. *The Life Aquatic with Steve Zissou* is a film about a selfish, unscrupulous man desperately trying to salvage his reputation. A man who wants to be loved but who shirks his responsibilities as a father and a husband, and abuses the trust of his most devoted supporters. When Zissou learns that Ned is not only his son but a proud member of the Zissou Society, he insists on taking him under his wing – not because he suddenly feels the need to make up for lost time, but because he sees in Ned someone who might provide a much-needed boost to his brittle ego. Nevertheless, just as Cousteau made amends by setting up the Cousteau Society in 1973 to encourage the exploration and protection of the world's aquatic ecosystems, Anderson ultimately throws his salty protagonist a redemptive lifeline.

ABOVE: The model of the *Belafonte* used in the scene where Steve Zissou gives a tour of the ship.

RIGHT: The *Calypso* during its heyday under Cousteau's captaincy.

OPPOSITE: Michelangelo's *La Madonna della Pietà* (1498–99; top left) and Francis Ford Coppola with his daughter Sofia (top right), which both inspired shots in *The Life Aquatic with Steve Zissou* (bottom).

FATHER AND SON

Towards the end of *The Life Aquatic with Steve Zissou*, Anderson alludes to two images that epitomize Zissou's redemption. The first is Michelangelo's *La Madonna della Pietà*, a marble sculpture enshrined within St Peter's Basilica, Vatican City, that portrays the Virgin Mary cradling the body of Jesus Christ following his crucifixion, a prominent visual theme in Southern Renaissance art. This pose is replicated in the scene where Zissou carries Ned out of the sea after their helicopter crash. The crash itself is edited in a similar style to a scene from Jean-Luc Godard's *Weekend* (1967), with disorienting block colour flash cuts.

The second image is a photograph of Francis Ford Coppola and his daughter Sofia, taken in May 1979 at the closing ceremony of the 32nd Cannes Film Festival. The American director had just received the Palme d'Or for *Apocalypse Now*, which he shared that year with German director Volker Schlöndorff for *The Tin Drum*. After his own successful premiere, Zissou is shown carrying Klaus' young nephew, Werner (Leonardo Giovannelli), on his shoulders down the red-carpeted steps leading away from the theatre. With Zissou in his tux and Werner in knee socks, and paparazzi flashbulbs bursting around them, it is both a sweet tribute and a satisfying way to round off *The Life Aquatic with Steve Zissou*'s main narrative arc.

'I GOT SCRUPLES TOO, YOU KNOW. YOU KNOW WHAT THAT IS? SCRUPLES?' – MOSES PRAY

OPPOSITE: Schemers and dreamers: Moses and Addie engage in a battle of wits en route to Missouri (top). In *Bottle Rocket*, Dignan reveals his big heist plan to a distracted Anthony in a Dallas diner (bottom), a scene also inspired by Martin Scorsese's *Goodfellas*.

PART 4
Paper Moon

(Peter Bogdanovich, 1973)

Anderson's films, particularly *The Royal Tenenbaums*, *Moonrise Kingdom*, *The Grand Budapest Hotel* (2014), *The French Dispatch* (2021) and *Asteroid City* (2023), are often interpreted as attempts to recapture moments in time. These moments typically represent attitudes, ideas and ways of life that are disappearing or have already vanished. Despite his retro leanings, however, Anderson never indulges in nostalgia for nostalgia's sake. The same could be said of Peter Bogdanovich, a filmmaker whom Anderson considers himself a student of.

In the early 1970s, Bogdanovich made a handful of films that can be described as elegies for a bygone America. Among them is *Paper Moon*, which was adapted by screenwriter Alvin Sargent from Joe David Brown's 1971 novel *Addie Pray*. Bogdanovich's charming, not-too-sentimental Depression-era caper combines elements of family drama, road movie and screwball comedy to tell the story of smooth-talking con artist Moses Pray (Ryan O'Neal), who makes a living by posing as a Bible salesman to swindle honest country folk out of their meagre savings.

Moses' devious ploy involves persuading widows to settle the outstanding balance on personalized copies of the Good Book their husbands supposedly ordered prior to their deaths. In order to pull this off, he must keep a low profile, but that changes when he meets nine-year-old Addie (played by Ryan O'Neal's real-life daughter, Tatum), newly orphaned

and suspicious that Moses is her real father. The pair, who naturally bear a close resemblance, do not see eye to eye at first. But Addie's neighbours convince Moses to drive her to her aunt's house in Missouri, and so they set off from rural Kansas in Moses' unreliable Ford Model A convertible, proceeding to bicker, blag and bluff their way across the Midwest.

Although Moses is not a 'bad dad', in the Royal Tenenbaum (Gene Hackman) or Steve Zissou mould, it's fair to say that he does not possess strong paternal instincts. In fact, at times he seems more childlike in appearance than his impish sidekick – *Paper Moon* is as much Moses' coming-of-age story as it is Addie's. In *Bottle Rocket*, Dignan is portrayed as an impetuous schemer who aspires to be a master criminal, while Anthony is just along for the ride. They are both grown men who behave like anything but; in other words, men like Moses. There are also traces of Moses and Addie's relationship in *The Grand Budapest Hotel*, with M. Gustave (Ralph Fiennes) and Zero (Tony Revolori) forging a similarly unlikely but tight bond, as noted in Chapter 4.

Over the course of *Bottle Rocket* and *The Grand Budapest Hotel*, the main characters all learn that it is better to keep moving forward than to constantly look back. *Paper Moon* shares the same sentiment. Much of the film's comedy stems from the sharp dialogue and sparkling chemistry between Ryan and Tatum O'Neal, not to mention the realization that Addie, despite her age and inexperience, is a more talented hustler than Moses is. The tragedy of *Paper Moon* lies in its historical setting. Far from offering a rose-tinted view of the past, Bogdanovich shows the extreme lengths people went to during the Great Depression to escape hardship. In this context, the final shot of Moses and Addie driving down a dusty, winding road to nowhere is particularly affecting. As long as they keep heading towards the horizon, anywhere will do.

There are a few more notable links between Bogdanovich and Anderson. First, it's worth noting that, aside from his own films, Anderson has produced just two narrative features to date: *The Squid and the Whale* (2005), directed by his good friend and frequent collaborator Noah Baumbach, and Bogdanovich's penultimate film, the screwball comedy *She's Funny That Way* (2014), which, not by chance, stars Owen Wilson in one of the lead roles. The part was originally written for John Ritter, but the actor's death in 2003 prompted Bogdanovich to shelve the project; it wasn't until Anderson introduced Bogdanovich to Wilson that he decided to revive the film.

Second, the church where Sam and Suzy first meet in *Moonrise Kingdom*, and where the townspeople take shelter during the climactic storm, was renamed St Jack's Church in honour of Bogdanovich's 1979 film *Saint Jack*. Writing about *Saint Jack* for *Sight and Sound* magazine in 1999, Anderson admitted to copying a scene featuring Ben Gazzarra's Jack Flowers and Bogdanovich's Eddie Schuman in *Bottle Rocket*:

> The two men get out of their car and walk through a park, discussing a deal, while the camera pulls back with them. At the end of their conversation, they turn around and return to the car; the camera, however, remains fixed, just watching them walk away. I liked this scene so much I stole the shot in my first film.

Third, Bogdanovich co-wrote his debut feature, *Targets* (1968), with his then-wife Polly Platt, who also served as the film's costume designer and production designer. Platt made significant contributions to Bogdanovich's most successful early works, *The Last Picture Show* (1971) and *What's Up, Doc?* (1972), and is widely credited with having discovered, among others, the actor Cybill Shepherd,

who got her break in *The Last Picture Show*. Unfortunately for Platt, Bogdanovich would eventually leave her for the emerging star. After Platt's separation from Bogdanovich, she continued to work off and on as a producer and was instrumental in helping Anderson develop *Bottle Rocket* into a full-length feature.

Anderson's decision to shoot *Bottle Rocket* in black-and-white was almost certainly informed, at least in part, by the expressive deep-focus cinematography of *The Last Picture Show* and *Paper Moon*, which were lensed by Robert Surtees and László Kovács, respectively. In each case, the rich monochrome enhances the overall evocation of not just a specific time period, but also the feeling of being in the moment. Elsewhere, *The Last Picture Show*'s sitcom-style end credits sequence has been repurposed by Anderson on several occasions, while his commercial short film *Castello Cavalcanti* (2013) contains a blink-and-you'll-miss-it reference to Addie.

OPPOSITE: The official US theatrical poster for *Paper Moon* (left), and the cover of Joe David Brown's 1971 source novel *Addie Pray* (right).

ABOVE: Polly Platt in conversation with Ryan O'Neal (top); and on the phone at her office at Paramount Pictures (bottom left).

Peter Bogdanovich directing Tatum O'Neal on the set of *Paper Moon* (bottom middle).

The tender moment when Moses realises his true paternal feelings towards Addie (bottom right).

PAPER MOON IS AS MUCH MOSES' COMING-OF-AGE STORY AS IT IS ADDIE'S

CHAPTER 6

CREATURE COMFORTS

'WHENEVER SOMEONE CREATES SOMETHING WITH ALL OF THEIR HEART, THEN THAT CREATION IS GIVEN A SOUL.' – HAYAO MIYAZAKI

OPPOSITE: Hugging it out: The moment when Mei and Satsuki are reunited in front of the Catbus (top) is matched by Anderson in *Isle of Dogs* when Atari embraces puppy protagonist Chief after a successful game of fetch (bottom).

PART 1
My Neighbor Totoro

(Hayao Miyazaki, 1988)

Animals, both wild and domesticated, play an important role in Anderson's films. Sometimes, they bridge emotional divides between characters, as seen with the goldfish Max (Jason Schwarzman) gifts to Miss Cross (Olivia Williams) in *Rushmore* (1998), or Buckley in *The Royal Tenenbaums* (2001), whose untimely demise brings Chas (Ben Stiller) closer to his father and sons. Other times, they signify a direct threat to human characters, as in the case of Cody the three-legged dog in *The Life Aquatic with Steve Zissou* (2004), Snoopy the scout mascot in *Moonrise Kingdom* (2012), or Kovacs' (Jeff Goldblum) cat in *The Grand Budapest Hotel* (2014). Anderson always places animals in a human context – even the feral protagonists of *Fantastic Mr. Fox* (2009) display anthropomorphic characteristics and are constantly imperilled by their proximity to men.

Isle of Dogs (2018) is an outlier in Anderson's filmography in that its story largely unfolds on a man-made refuse site far from civilization which has been transformed into a canine colony with its own self-determining rules and rituals. Here, a human character puts themselves at risk by entering the animals' domain, not the other way around. In this sense, the film evokes *My Neighbor Totoro*, Hayao Miyazaki's second feature as director for the beloved Japanese animation house Studio Ghibli, which concerns two young girls who move to the countryside with their father to be closer to their sick mother. There, four-year-old Mei (voiced by Chika Sakamoto) and her elder sister Satsuki

(Noriko Hidaka) are drawn to an enchanted forest filled with all kinds of strange and wonderful creatures.

Speaking at New York's Metrograph theatre in 2018, Anderson recalled that he started getting into Miyazaki around the time he was making *Fantastic Mr. Fox*. However, it wasn't until he visited the Ghibli Museum in Mitaka, Japan, that he became fully engrossed in Miyazaki's miraculous hand-crafted world:

> While I was there, I bought all the [Studio Ghibli] movies. I still watch them; I show my daughter them. In a movie like *Totoro*, two-thirds of the movie is spent on cleaning up the house, just wandering around the property, getting to know the neighbours, taking a bath . . . It's a very different kind of rhythm and emphasis from what you would ever see in an American animated movie.

At the world premiere of *Isle of Dogs* one month prior, Anderson explained precisely what drew him to *My Neighbor Totoro*:

> With Miyazaki, you get nature and you get moments of peace . . . That inspired us quite a lot. There were times when I worked with [composer] Alexandre Desplat on the score and we found many places where we had to pull back from what we were doing musically because the movie wanted to be quiet. That came from Miyazaki.

Silence and stillness permeate *Isle of Dogs* more than any other Anderson film. It's the moment of calm before sumo wrestlers' clash. The brief pause before a sushi chef grabs a pinch of wasabi poison. The hush that falls when a young boy recites an impassioned *haiku* during a live televised debate. In a 2002 interview with the late American film critic Roger Ebert, Miyazaki spoke about the Japanese concept of *ma* (which roughly translates to 'emptiness' or 'negative space') in relation to the points in his films where time appears to slow down; where the action in a scene is given room to breathe. Anderson may not be a direct apprentice to Miyazaki, but watching *Isle of Dogs* it's clear that he has learned a thing or two from the old master.

Miyazaki is also noted for his environmentalism. He has often examined humanity's relationship with nature and the spirit world as expressed in Japan's indigenous belief system, *Shinto* (meaning 'way of the gods'). In *My Neighbor Totoro*, Mei and Satsuki learn about the powerful yet finely balanced forces of nature not by reading about them in school, but by experiencing them firsthand. The spellbinding nighttime scene where the sisters, with a little help from the Totoros, conjure a mighty Camphor tree – a recurring motif in the film – from a few seedlings, willing it to grow until it towers above the landscape, is presented as a dream. Yet Miyazaki makes it seem as real to us as it does to Mei and Satsuki; even when they awake the next morning to find the tree gone, the magic doesn't wear off.

Despite the film's near-future timeline and Megasaki City being a made-up metropolis, *Isle of Dogs* is firmly rooted in current real-world ecological concerns. Its primary setting is a vast wasteland occupied by living beings that have been disposed of by Megasaki's human population like so much floating junk. In an interview with the *Hollywood Reporter* around the time of the film's release, production designer Adam Stockhausen stated that Trash Island was designed to represent 'the way in which a society chooses to put its own crisis of waste removal out of sight and therefore out of mind ... The dogs can be seen as representing any group of dispossessed beings, be they human or not.'

This chimes with the suggestion in many of Miyazaki's films, particularly *My Neighbor Totoro*, that people, particularly those who live in built-up urban areas, are largely ignorant of the harm they cause to nature, and, by

extension, each other. Like Miyazaki, Anderson doesn't force his environmental agenda upon the viewer. Yet both *My Neighbor Totoro* and *Isle of Dogs* raise urgent questions about our attitudes towards nature and why its capacity to adapt and regenerate only seems to arouse humanity's worst impulses.

Two more Japanese animated works that influenced *Isle of Dogs* were Katsuhiro Otomo's *Akira* (1988) and Hideaki Anno's anime series *Neon Genesis Evangelion* (1995–96), both of which depict dystopian visions of a futuristic Tokyo. There are also parallels with Miyazaki's *Porco Rosso* (1992), namely in the form of its porcine protagonist whose aerial abilities stand in stark contrast to Atari's (Koyu Rankin), who crash-lands a stolen plane on Trash Island while searching for his lost dog.

In a final nod to Miyazaki, actor Mari Natsuki is listed among *Isle of Dogs'* cast as 'Auntie', the elderly host of Greta Gerwig's American exchange student-turned-political activist, Tracy. Natsuki previously appeared in the Japanese director's 2001 film *Spirited Away* in the twin roles of Yubaba and Zeniba, who teach the lead character Chihiro (Rumi Hiiragi) that the world contains both good and evil, and that it's not always easy to spot the difference between them.

RIGHT: The official Japanese theatrical poster for *My Neighbor Totoro*.

ABOVE: The dramatic explosion on Trash Island (top) carries an echo of the apocalyptic opening scene of *Akira* (bottom).

RIGHT: The frilly collared Shih Tzu that appears early on in *Isle of Dogs* (top) is a facsimile of Ohara Koson's *ukiyo-e* style painting from the 1930s (bottom).

FAR RIGHT: Hayao Miyazaki in front of his studio in Koganei, Tokyo.

ABOVE: Another famous piece of Japanese art recreated for the film is Katsushika Hokusai's *The Great Wave off Kanagawa* (top), a woodblock print dating from the Edo period. In Anderson's version, numerous dogs are depicted riding the wave (bottom).

OPPOSITE: *Oxford tire pile #8, Westley, CA, USA*, shot by Canadian photographer Edward Burtynsky in 1999 (top left), was among the key reference images for Trash Island (top right and bottom).

TWO MEN'S TRASH

While *Isle of Dogs* takes its visual cues from various sources, from the films of Hayao Miyazaki and Akira Kurosawa to traditional Japanese *ukiyo-e* art by the likes of Katsushika Hokusai, the main influence for Trash Island was the work of two environmental photographers who have spent much of their careers documenting industrial landscapes and the far-reaching impacts of mass consumption. As Paul Harrod, one of the film's production designers, explained to the online magazine *Atlas Obscura* in 2018: 'Edward Burtynsky and Chris Jordan have been documenting the crisis of trash we are facing right now, how there already exists these vast landscapes of trash.'

Together with Adam Stockhausen, Harrod studied Burtynsky's Anthropocene and Urban Mines collections, as well as Jordan's Intolerable Beauty series, closely examining the colours, textures, composition and scale of their large-format images. In a different interview with the *Hollywood Reporter*, Harrod elaborated:

What was interesting about these two photographers was that their images were nightmarish and oppressive, while also having a perverse sort of aesthetic appeal. The intent was for Trash Island to always have that quality; to be captivating in the way only a vision of Hell can be.

'FLY, KES. FLY LIKE THE WIND!' – BILLY CASPAR

OPPOSITE: Birds of a feather: The close bond formed between Billy and Kes (top) gave Anderson the idea for Richie Tenenbaum's pet falcon Mordecai (bottom).

PART 2
Kes

(Ken Loach, 1969)

Adapted from Barry Hines' 1968 novel *A Kestrel for a Knave*, Ken Loach's breakthrough feature is a hardscrabble coming-of-age story about a boy and his bird. Set in Barnsley in the north of England, the film centres on a working-class teenager named Billy (David Bradley) who routinely gets into trouble at school with his teachers and classmates, and at home with his long-suffering single mother (Lynne Perrie) and brutish older half-brother, Jud (Freddie Fletcher). *Kes* is often remembered as a quintessential British 'kitchen sink' drama. Despite its unvarnished visual style and socially conscious themes, however, there are times when the story reaches a transcendent, almost dreamlike state.

Indeed, while Loach is synonymous with a particularly austere brand of cinematic realism, some scenes in *Kes* could just as easily belong to a fairy tale. Early in the film, Billy is shown wandering through a dense patch of woods on the edge of town. The musical score is light and optimistic as Billy clears a path through the undergrowth with a stick, inspects a rather large mushroom and hurls a log into a pond. He stops at a clearing and looks up in awe at a pair of kestrels darting across the sky. It is a moment of pure cinematic wonder simultaneously tinged with sadness because we sense that Billy will never be as free as those birds.

The central human-animal relationship features less than one might expect from the title. Still, the scenes with Billy and Kes are among the most memorable in the film, providing welcome respite, however fleetingly, from the grim realities of life in a poor mining town. Moreover, while Billy endures a miserable time at school, his burgeoning hobby at once reveals an innate curiosity and a fondness for learning and reading.

After plucking Kes from a nest in a crumbling farm building, Billy attempts to borrow a book from his local library with a view to raising the young bird but is turned away for not having a membership. So, he goes to a nearby bookstore and steals a copy of M.H. Woodford's *A Manual of Falconry* – the kind of specialist-interest handbook you might expect to pop up in one of Anderson's films. At several points in the film, Billy is shown narrating passages from the book over images of him training and caring for Kes.

Of course, books are a core component of Anderson's world-building. *The Royal Tenenbaums* opens with a shot of an eponymous biography by the fictional author W.R. Wales being checked out of a library; the hands that stamp the card inside the cover belonging to Anderson. In *Fantastic Mr. Fox*, a clay model of a human hand, which could well also be the director's, holds up a first edition copy of Dahl's book with what appears to be a library sticker on its spine. Many of Anderson's protagonists are avid readers and, as with *Kes*, literature is often a source of comfort or inspiration for his young characters. For example, Margot Tenenbaum's (Gwyneth Paltrow) bedroom boasts its own mini library stocked with collected plays by the likes of Beckett, Chekhov and Pinter. And in *Moonrise Kingdom*, Suzy (Kara Hayward) packs a suitcase full of books for her and Sam's (Jared Gilman) expedition.

Like most boys his age, Billy also loves comics. In a light-hearted moment of boyhood escapism, Billy takes a break from his paper round and sits down with a copy of the long-running children's weekly comic *The Dandy* on a grassy bank overlooking a smoking coal refinery. He reads Desperate Dan's latest adventure out loud as the camera hops from panel to panel. The playful humour and quirky editing of this scene have become Anderson's stock in trade, and it's possible that the American action comic that Ash (voiced by Jason Schwartzman) is shown reading in *Fantastic Mr. Fox* ('White Cape vs. the Black Dog', which was created for the film by Anderson and storyboard artist Christian De Vita), is an oblique reference to *Kes*.

Out of all of Anderson's films, *The Royal Tenenbaums* has the most in common with *Kes*. It's easy to picture Richie (Luke Wilson) and Mordecai as a grown-up version of Billy and Kes, albeit in a very different context and setting. Yet the characters' fates are opposed. In Loach's film, Billy is left distraught when he comes home to find that Jud has killed Kes and dumped the bird's body in a dustbin – a vicious act of retaliation for his brother's failure to place a bet on his behalf. In contrast, Mordecai's unexpected return symbolizes that Richie's emotional scars are starting to heal. When he and Margot reconcile on top of the Tenenbaum house at the end of the film, Mordecai is right there with him. In the director's commentary, Anderson reveals that he snuck Mordecai's caw into the sound mix at various points in the film to suggest that the bird remains a constant presence in Richie's life even after it is set free. If *Kes* is about the possibility of escape, then *The Royal Tenenbaums* is about making peace with the life – and family – you have.

In a further echo of *Kes*, the sudden death of Chas Tenenbaum's pet dog, Buckley, prompts him to reassess his excessive risk-averseness, ultimately leading to him patching things up with his pa. It's also highly likely that Chas's sportswear was inspired by Billy's sadistic PE teacher, Mr Sugden (Brian Glover), who wears a red tracksuit during the famous football match scene. Elsewhere, although Anderson has stated that a different Loach film, *Black Jack*

(1979), had a greater influence on *Moonrise Kingdom* than *Kes*, there are certain similarities between Billy and Sam. As the original UK theatrical poster for *Kes* states: 'Both wild . . . both alike in their love of freedom and contemptuous of the world around them.'

Billy is a misfit and a dreamer who is determined to make something of himself despite the odds being stacked against him: 'I'm not gonna work down t'pit,' he repeatedly insists. In this sense, he could comfortably fit into Anderson's world alongside Dignan (Owen Wilson), Max, the Tenenbaum children, Mr Fox (voiced by George Clooney), Sam and Suzy, M. Gustave (Ralph Fiennes) and Zero (Tony Revolori). But more important than any corresponding character traits or narrative details found in Anderson and Loach's work is the directors' shared understanding of the power of cinema to transport an audience. Like the first time we see the kestrels soaring above Billy's head, the climax of *The Royal Tenenbaums*' prologue, when Mordecai takes flight in sync to the Mutato Muzika Orchestra's cover of the Beatles' 'Hey Jude' (2014), is nothing short of euphoric.

LEFT: Chas's tracksuit in *The Royal Tenenbaums* (top) is reminiscent of the burgundy number worn by Mr Sugden (bottom) during the famous football match scene in *Kes*.

OPPOSITE: The official UK quad poster for *Kes* (top).

The fictional superhero comic that Ash is seen reading (middle left) could be a subtle reference to the scene where Billy immerses himself in a copy of *The Dandy* (bottom left).

David Bradley and Ken Loach share a happy moment on the set of the film (bottom right).

"Both wild...both alike in their love of freedom and contemptuous of the world around them!

He called the Kestrel

Kes

...as he would a friend.

Woodfall Films present A Kestrel Films Production "KES" U starring DAVID BRADLEY
From Barry Hines' book "Kestrel For A Knave" Adapted by BARRY HINES, KEN LOACH & TONY GARNETT Produced by TONY GARNETT Directed by KEN LOACH

'I DON'T WANT TO LIVE IN A HOLE ANYMORE,
AND I'M GOING TO DO SOMETHING ABOUT IT.' – MR FOX

OPPOSITE: Room to write: Anderson based the design of the study where Mr Fox reveals his plan to Kylie (bottom) on the famous hut where Roald Dahl wrote many of his stories (top).

PART 3
Fantastic Mr Fox

(Roald Dahl, 1970)

Roald Dahl's *Fantastic Mr Fox* was published one year after Anderson was born, and he has described it as the first book he remembers owning as a child. Anderson visited Gipsy House, Dahl's estate in Great Missenden, Buckinghamshire, for the first time in the early 2000s as a guest of the author's widow, Felicity, and signed on to adapt *Fantastic Mr Fox* with Noah Baumbach a few years later. In 2023, Anderson directed a series of short Dahl adaptations for Netflix: *The Wonderful Story of Henry Sugar, Poison, The Ratcatcher* and *The Swan*.

While writing the script for *Fantastic Mr. Fox*, Anderson and Baumbach moved into Gipsy House to fully immerse themselves in Dahl's world. As a result, the film retains many of Dahl's individual quirks, along with entire portions of his idiosyncratic prose. The descriptions of Boggis (voiced by Robin Hurlstone), Bunce (voiced by Hugo Guiness) and Bean (voiced by Helen McCrory), one weighing 'the same as a young rhinoceros,' the next 'approximately the size of a pot-bellied dwarf' whose 'chin would be under water at

the shallow end of any pool on the planet', and the other 'as skinny as a pencil, as smart as a whip, and possibly the scariest man currently living', are lifted almost word-for-word from the book.

When Mr Fox explains his masterplan to pull off one last raid of Boggis's chicken house, he's seated in a wingback chair with a writing table laid across the armrests and an Anglepoise lamp for light, mimicking the set-up of Dahl's writing shed. In a promotional 'making of' featurette, Felicity Dahl revealed that Anderson had every object and piece of furniture in Gipsy House photographed and then had miniatures made of them. So, the Fox home that we see in the film is in essence Dahl's; even the large beech tree that the Fox family moves into was modelled on one at the top of the author's garden.

When designing the characters and storyboards, Anderson was greatly influenced by Donald Chaffin, who illustrated the first edition of *Fantastic Mr Fox*, particularly his symmetrical compositions and use of cross-sectional perspective. In fact, Anderson hired Chaffin as a consultant on *Fantastic Mr. Fox*, which explains why so many scenes resemble his drawings; the book cover that appears at the start of the film bears an unmistakable likeness to Chaffin's original. There are also hints of Jill Bennett's vivid illustrations from the UK first edition, not to mention Quentin Blake's simpler yet more kinetic style. More than anything, though, *Fantastic Mr. Fox* is infused with the spirit of Chaffin's work – just look at Mr Fox's dapper attire, the nonchalant way Rat (Willem Dafoe) swills cider from the top shelf of Bean's cider store, or how Mrs Fox (Meryl Streep) tenderly patches up her newly tailless husband.

The film also features plenty of original artwork. Anderson enlisted the services of environment designer Turlo Griffin, who has since worked on *Isle of Dogs*, *Asteroid City* (2023) and *The Wonderful Story of Henry Sugar*, to create the huge mural and moody landscape paintings Mrs Fox is shown working on, as well as character concept art and several matte backgrounds; the townscape and other details of the mural were added by painter and modeller Roy Bell. The heroic group portrait hanging in Clive Badger, Esq.'s (Bill Murray) office is reminiscent of a historic military painting and subtly reinforces the power dynamic between Mr Fox and his combustible lawyer.

TOP: Anderson's film opens with an anonymous character holding Dahl's book aloft (left), which closely resembles Donald Chaffin's real-world illustration for the first edition cover (right).

BOTTOM: Dahl relaxing in his writing chair (left) at his home in Great Missenden in 1980, known as Gipsy House (right).

OPPOSITE: The painting seen hanging in Badger's office (bottom) is intended to evoke classical military paintings, such as Philip James de Loutherbourg's 1802 artwork *The Battle of Alexandria, 21 March 1801* (top).

Crucially, the ending of *Fantastic Mr. Fox* differs from the book. In Dahl's version, Mr Fox finally outwits his human nemeses by digging a network of tunnels leading directly to their storehouses, securing a lasting supply of food for his family and the wider woodland community. In Anderson's version, he breaks into an even more well-stocked supermarket owned by the three farmers. This is foreshadowed in the whack-bat scene when a plane flies overhead carrying a banner advertising 'Boggis, Bunce and Bean International Supermarkets'. Interestingly, the film's ending was taken from an earlier manuscript. Dahl had to change his original ending at the request of his US publishers, who felt that an assault on a supermarket could be interpreted as an anti-capitalist message by more conservative readers.

Despite being faithful to both Dahl and Chaffin, *Fantastic Mr. Fox* has its own distinctive style. Anderson took a certain amount of creative licence to ensure that his artistic voice cut through, from the strictly autumnal colour scheme which features virtually no blue or green, to the inclusion of various Americanisms such as an opossum (a species native to North America), the baseball-esque game of whack-bat and the Action 12 news crew. Additionally, the four Fox children are replaced in the film by Ash (Jason Schwartzman) and his cousin Kristofferson (Eric Chase Anderson), who was named after the American actor and musician Kris Kristofferson.

By adding secondary characters and making significant alterations to others, Anderson expands on Dahl's story while allying the author's worldview with his own. As a result, many of the director's familiar thematic concerns are brought to the forefront: Kristofferson's natural athletic ability earns him the admiration of his uncle, while Ash's attempts to impress his father go largely unnoticed; Mr Fox is introduced to the sound of 'The Ballad of Davy Crockett', as performed by the Wellingtons for the 1954 Disney mini-series *Davy Crockett*, setting him up as a boyish frontiersman more in the vein of Sam Shakusky or Eli Cash than Dahl's fearless but level-headed patriarch.

Later, during the daring rescue sequence, Mr Fox rides a vintage sidecar motorcycle while wearing a black balaclava and old-fashioned racing goggles. In a 2009 *New Yorker* profile, Anderson stated that he:

. . . wanted to make a children's movie like some of the ones I grew up with. And that went with the idea of how you didn't have to wear helmets when you rode bicycles. I never wore a helmet riding a bicycle, and, in a way, the movie is for children who don't wear helmets when they ride bicycles.

Still, if Anderson's Mr Fox is portrayed as a rebel with a cause, he is above all a protector, just as Dahl wrote him. While this archetype was largely absent from Anderson's work pre-*Fantastic Mr. Fox*, it has since become a staple of it.

BY ADDING SECONDARY CHARACTERS AND MAKING SIGNIFICANT ALTERATIONS TO OTHERS, ANDERSON EXPANDS ON DAHL'S STORY WHILE ALLYING THE AUTHOR'S WORLDVIEW WITH HIS OWN

OPPOSITE: Anderson making an adjustment to a puppet on the set of *Fantastic Mr. Fox* (top). The hand-crafted look of the models (bottom right) was partly inspired by traditional stop-motion animations such as *Le roman de Renard* from 1937 (bottom left).

STOP-MOTION MAGIC

Initially, Anderson envisioned *Fantastic Mr. Fox* as a collaboration with filmmaker Henry Selick, who had previously animated the Rankin/Bass-inspired sea creatures in *The Life Aquatic with Steve Zissou*. Before that, Selick directed an adaptation of Dahl's *James and the Giant Peach*, combining live-action and stop-motion, and scored a hit in 1993 with *The Nightmare Before Christmas*, based on an original concept by Tim Burton. Selick left *Fantastic Mr. Fox* after his own project, *Coraline*, was greenlit, and was replaced as animation director by Mark Gustafson, who cut his teeth on *Return to Oz* (1985) and more recently co-directed *Guillermo del Toro's Pinocchio* (2022).

Aside from owing an obvious debt to Selick, Anderson has stated that *Fantastic Mr. Fox* was partly inspired by stop-motion pioneer Władysław Starewicz's first fully animated feature, *Le roman de Renard* (*The Tale of the Fox*, 1937). The film was made with the assistance of the director's daughter, Irene, over an 18-month period ending in 1930, but it was not released until 1937 due to a delay in obtaining funding for a soundtrack. Recounting the exploits of a cunning and mischievous fox who comes into conflict with a noble lion king, *Le roman de Renard* is notable for its innovative use of a wide array of props and puppets of varying sizes, from miniatures to full-scale models.

'BE CUNNING AND FULL OF TRICKS AND YOUR PEOPLE SHALL NEVER BE DESTROYED.' – RICHARD ADAMS, *WATERSHIP DOWN*

OPPOSITE: Green and pleasant land: The hand-painted rolling hills that appear in *Watership Down* (top) were a big influence on the landscape imagery in *Fantastic Mr. Fox* (bottom).

PART 4
Watership Down

(Martin Rosen, 1978)

Richard Adams' classic children's novel *Watership Down* was published two years after Dahl's *Fantastic Mr Fox*; combining elements of fantasy and oral folklore, it tells the story of a group of rabbits who embark on a perilous journey through the bucolic English countryside. Both the book and director Martin Rosen's subsequent film adaptation depict the ruthless exploitation and destruction of the natural world by humankind, a theme in Anderson's own animated films, *Fantastic Mr. Fox* and *Isle of Dogs*. When asked to name his all-time favourite animated film in an interview with the French magazine *Purple* in 2009, Anderson replied without hesitation: *Watership Down*.

As in *Fantastic Mr. Fox*, the lapine protagonists of *Watership Down* find sanctuary on a quiet hilltop crowned with a single tree. Here, Hazel (voiced by John Hurt), his brother Fiver (Richard Briers) and their intrepid followers make a new home for themselves, having fled their previous warren in light of one of Fiver's eerie premonitions. Although they clash with numerous natural predators, as well as their own kind (it's entirely plausible that the total cost of child therapy sessions linked to General Woundwort – voiced by Harry Andrews – following *Watership Down*'s release far outweighed the film's budget), man is by far the greatest threat to our heroes' survival. Adams always insisted that his story was 'just about rabbits', but its allegorical overtones are hard to ignore.

Rosen purchased the film rights to *Watership Down* in 1976 for a reported £50,000 and started work on production soon after. He brought in veteran American animator John Hubley and set up shop in an old tanning factory in central London (on Warren Street, no less), a large enough space to accommodate all the different animation departments. Rosen briefly considered using poseable puppets before deciding that a traditional animated approach would best serve the story. Hubley, however, was fired part-way through production after falling out with Rosen. He died during heart surgery in 1977 and never saw the completed film, but his legacy survives in the moving epilogue sequence where an older Hazel is greeted by the rabbit spirit El-ahrairah.

The idyllic scenery of *Watership Down* was inspired by the illustrations and maps found in the original novel, which Adams drew from real locations around the Hampshire Downs near his hometown of Newbury. Yet the film's naturalistic tone was enhanced not only by its gorgeous watercolour palette but also its organic sound design. Editor Terry Rawlings and sound mixer Ray Merrin visited the actual Watership Down to record the dawn chorus, as well as atmospheric sounds from the exact railway bridge and river mentioned in the book.

Anderson adopted a similar approach for *Fantastic Mr. Fox*, instructing the sound department to capture field recordings of animal noises and various natural sounds. In addition, the film's sound design pays close attention to the characters' environment. For example, when the action takes place underground, the acoustics are noticeably more claustrophobic and echoey, a technique borrowed from *Watership Down*. Anderson also opted not to record the dialogue in a professional studio, instead bringing most of the principal cast to a friend's farm in Connecticut where they performed their parts in barns, stables, next to streams and in nearby woodland, adding to the film's rustic texture.

Rosen adapted another of Adams' novels four years later: the biting political satire *The Plague Dogs* (1982). Employing a similar if more muted animation style, the film follows a grizzled black Labrador mix named Rowf (Christopher Benjamin) and a plucky fox terrier named Snitter (John Hurt) who break out of an animal laboratory near Coniston in the Lake District. Free from the clutches of 'the white coats' and their wicked experiments, the dogs make for the hills, but soon find themselves fighting for survival in an unfamiliar and unforgiving landscape. What begins as a tale of liberation descends into tragedy as the pair becomes embroiled in a national scandal (unbeknownst to them) that reaches all the way up to the House of Commons.

Anderson has cited *The Plague Dogs* as a key inspiration for *Isle of Dogs*. In the latter film, the entire canine population of a fictional Japanese city is banished to a garbage-covered archipelago following the outbreak of 'snout fever', a highly contagious virus that is thought to be transmittable to humans. According to a 2018 interview with *Little White Lies* magazine, Anderson got the idea for Trash Island from several TV shows he watched as a child, including *Fat Albert and the Cosby Kids*, *Sesame Street* and *Sanford and Son*. In Rosen's film, the escaped hounds incur the wrath not just of the local farmers whose sheep they kill for sustenance, but also the UK government, which has reason to believe they may be carrying bubonic plague. Both films include scenes of humans laying siege to the unsuspecting dogs from above, although the effect is much less harrowing in Anderson's.

During the press conference for *Isle of Dogs* at the 2018 Berlin International Film Festival, Anderson revealed that Noah Baumbach introduced him to *The Plague Dogs*, describing it as a 'very, very bleak movie'. Bleak is something of an understatement. Yet while Anderson's film is ostensibly an adventure comedy, it too does not shy away from the cruelty man's best friend is sometimes subjected to, as evidenced by the presence on Trash Island of an animal testing facility. *The Plague Dogs* is not entirely without hope, though. The devastating final scene ends on an unexpectedly life-affirming note, thanks in no small part to the empathetic performances of Benjamin and Hurt.

Rosen had a knack for pairing established actors with animated characters, and Anderson is equally adept in this department; although noted for his loyalty to certain actors, he often adds new voices to his regular roster with great success. Bryan Cranston in *Isle of Dogs* is a prime example: as the gruff-but-loveable stray Chief, he gives the film its emotional anchor. While we're on the subject of vocal performance, Kehaar (the black-headed gull in *Watership Down*) was voiced by Zero Mostel in what would be his final film role; Anderson naming Tony Revolori's character in *The Grand Budapest Hotel* after the larger-than-life American actor and comedian.

TOP: *Watership Down* voice actor Zero Mostel.

BOTTOM: *Watership Down* author Richard Adams was inspired by the verdant countryside near his home in Hampshire, England.

RIGHT: The canine protagonists of *The Plague Dogs* meet a watery end (top), while Atari, Chief and Spots find themselves swimming for their lives as they bid to get back to the mainland (middle).

The first edition paperback cover of *Watership Down* (bottom left); the official theatrical poster for the film adaptation (bottom middle); and the theatrical poster for *The Plague Dogs* (bottom right).

MAN IS BY FAR THE GREATEST THREAT TO OUR HEROES' SURVIVAL

CHAPTER 7

LIFE AND
DEATH

'I JUST CAN'T DIE . . . I DON'T KNOW WHAT I'VE BEEN
LIVING FOR ALL THESE YEARS.' – KANJI

OPPOSITE: Panel vision: Kurosawa frequently framed characters through open panels or windows in *shoji* screens (top), creating an isolating effect which Anderson replicates on several occasions in *The Grand Budapest Hotel* (bottom).

PART 1
Ikiru

(*To Live*, Akira Kurosawa, 1952)

Although Anderson's films are broadly comic in tone, tragedy is never far away. His characters are prone to accidental or premature death, typically by drowning, electrocution or poisoning. Sometimes they attempt suicide or commit murder. They frequently experience bereavement, with maternal absence a particularly prominent theme. In *Rushmore* (1998), Max's (Jason Schwartzman) mother's epitaph reads 'The paths of glory lead but to the grave', a line taken from Thomas Gray's 1751 poem 'Elegy Written in a Country Churchyard'. Similarly, *The Royal Tenenbaums* (2001) ends where *The Grand Budapest Hotel* (2014) begins: in a graveyard.

In *The Life Aquatic with Steve Zissou* (2004), our beanie-wearing hero's (Bill Murray) high-stakes mission to hunt down the jaguar shark is motivated by loss; by the time Zissou finally comes face to face with his white whale once more, ready to avenge his fallen comrade, his sense of grief has doubled. In *The Grand Budapest Hotel*, both M. Gustave (Ralph Fiennes) and Agatha (Saoirse Ronan) are killed off screen: the former shot by a fascist firing squad; the latter succumbing to 'Prussian grippe', 'an absurd little disease', Mr Moustafa (F. Murray Abraham) laments, that is now easily treatable. And in *Isle of Dogs* (2018), Professor Watanabe (Akira Ito) is poisoned for discovering a cure for dog flu, effectively turning him into a martyr for all dogkind.

Akira Kurosawa's influence on *Isle of Dogs*, especially regarding the subject of mortality, is as conspicuous as the toxic heap that makes up Trash Island's skyline. As well

as being a pun on 'I love dogs', the title of Anderson's film ostensibly alludes to *Stray Dog* (1949), in which Kurosawa mainstay Toshirô Mifune plays a rookie detective who wades into post-war Tokyo's criminal underworld after misplacing his service pistol. There's also a passing reference in *Isle of Dogs* to a 'Toho Mountain Ryokan', presumably in ode to Toho Co., the pioneering Japanese film studio that produced the original *Godzilla* (1954) films along with many of Kurosawa's best-known works, including *Seven Samurai* (1954), *Throne of Blood* (1957) and *Yojimbo* (1961).

Speaking of *Seven Samurai*, there are a couple of shots in *Isle of Dogs* that are directly lifted from Kurosawa's sixteenth-century epic. Meanwhile, composer Alexandre Desplat reworked several cues from Fumio Hayasaka's original score for the same film, in addition to reappropriating a piece of music from *Drunken Angel* (1948); the latter, along with *Dodes'ka-den* (1970), is set in a Tokyo slum. Elsewhere, *Isle of Dogs*' main antagonist, Mayor Kobayashi (voiced by Kunichi Nomura), was based on the lead characters from two of Kurosawa's most acclaimed crime dramas, *The Bad Sleep Well* (1960) and *High and Low* (1963), both played by Mifune; Anderson named Chief's owner Toshiro as a tribute to the Japanese screen icon.

Anderson's fascination with the passage of time, his use of long takes, and the importance he places on music in his films have all been influenced to some extent by Kurosawa, while his obsession with death and legacy can be specifically traced back to *Ikiru* (*To Live*). Inspired by Leo

Tolstoy's 1886 novella *The Death of Ivan Ilyich*, Kurosawa's deeply affecting drama centres on an ageing city councillor named Kanji Watanabe (Takashi Shimura), who, at the start of the film, is diagnosed with stomach cancer and given just six months to live. Upon learning his fate, which he keeps to himself, Watanabe suddenly realizes that he has been sleepwalking through life – his colleagues nickname him 'the Mummy' – and so he sets out to find new meaning in the short time he has left.

The film's English-translated title is *To Live*, and Watanabe is determined to do just that. At first, he squanders his time and money in Tokyo's sleaziest bars and nightclubs, partly to spite his only son, who cares more about his inheritance than his old man's wellbeing. Watanabe gambles and drinks, but nothing seems to ease his existential pain. So, he changes tack, arranging a lunch date with a high-spirited young woman from work after bumping into her on the street. Yet that only leaves him feeling lonelier and more useless. Finally, Watanabe has an epiphany. He uses his position as a senior bureaucrat with nothing to lose to force through the construction of a children's playground on a derelict site in one of the poorest parts of the city, something that will bring joy to people long after he is gone.

At Watanabe's wake, which takes up the last hour or so of the film, his former colleagues get drunk and argue over whether he knew about his illness and to what extent he should be given credit for the playground. In the end, it doesn't matter what anyone else thinks. A flashback to Watanabe's last night on Earth shows him swinging alone in the playground, singing a sad yet comforting tune to himself in the snow; the climbing structure in the foreground creating a literal frame within a frame. When the camera cuts to a front-on view of Watanabe, the look of contentment on his face tells us he has found what he was searching for. This shot, along with others in *Ikiru*, such as Watanabe's cluttered office and two characters glimpsed through a window in a *shoji* panel, have clearly inspired Anderson.

In 2018, shortly before the release of *Isle of Dogs*, Anderson co-curated a Kurosawa retrospective at New York's Metrograph Theater. The six films in the programme were *Drunken Angel*, *Stray Dog*, *Ikiru*, *I Live in Fear* (1955), *The Bad Sleep Well* and *High and Low*. Anderson said in his introduction to the season:

To people who love movies, Japan immediately conjures up the work of Akira Kurosawa: a cinematic *sensei* to generations of directors. If *Isle of Dogs* permits me an opportunity to present a few of the Master's masterpieces in 35mm (which were on our minds and in our DVD players every day of the creating of this movie), I am grateful for it.

LEFT: Toshirô Mifune as high-flying executive Kingo Gondo in Kurosawa's 1963 film *High and Low*. The character was one of several played by Mifune that influenced the look of *Isle of Dogs*' villain, Mayor Kobayashi.

OPPOSITE: A Japanese postcard for the Imperial Hotel in Tokyo (top), a building designed by Frank Lloyd Wright, which Anderson reconfigures as Mayor Kobayashi's Brick Mansion residence (bottom).

THE WRIGHT STUFF

According to Paul Harrod, co-production designer on *Isle of Dogs*, Mayor Kobayashi's palatial residence was based on the second iteration of Tokyo's Imperial Hotel, which was designed in the Maya Revival style by Frank Lloyd Wright and constructed between 1919 and 1923. 'We liked how it represented a fusion of traditional Japanese architecture with twentieth-century modernism,' Harrod told *Dezeen* in 2018:

> While the roof lines suggest an Edo-period design, the structure itself is masonry rather than wood, and the footprint suggests a western-styled plan. Wright has always been appealing to production designers because his use of strong horizontal lines and layers are well served by a wide-aspect ratio, but we actually went a bit more vertical with it to give it a more looming presence.

Another of Frank Lloyd Wright's famous buildings to have featured in one of Anderson's films is the John Gillin Residence in Dallas. Built in 1958 in Wright's signature Usonian style, this sprawling single-storey property was used as Bob Mapplethorpe's (Robert Musgrave) house in *Bottle Rocket* (1996), and was the last private residence designed by the celebrated architect. Before his death in 1959, Wright also designed the Kalita Humphreys Theater in Dallas, which has yet to make an appearance in an Anderson film, but which the director would have almost certainly visited during his time living in Texas.

'WE ALL HAVE INSIDE OURSELVES A WOMAN WHO WALKS ALONE ON THE ROAD.' – AGNÈS VARDA

OPPOSITE: Wanderlust: The long tracking shots repeatedly used by Varda to show Mona's journey (top) are copied in *Moonrise Kingdom* in the scene where Sam and Suzy meet up to elope (bottom).

PART 2
Vagabond

(Agnès Varda, 1985)

In 2022, Anderson included Agnès Varda's *Vagabond* among his ten favourite films of all time as part of *Sight and Sound*'s once-a-decade directors' poll. He exclusively selected French titles — not a huge surprise coming from the Paris-based, openly Francophile filmmaker. Varda's award-winning drama opens with an establishing shot of a windswept field in southern France, where a farmer discovers a frozen corpse slumped in a ditch. Police arrive on the scene, taking pictures of the young woman's body, emptying her pockets to make a record of her possessions, and packing her into a plastic bag as a matter of dispassionate protocol.

The director herself offers an elegiac assessment of the situation in voiceover, simultaneously setting up the film's pseudo-documentary approach:

No one claimed the body, so it went from a ditch to a potter's field. She had died a natural death without leaving a trace. I wonder if those who knew her as a child still think about her. But people she had met recently remembered her. Those witnesses helped me to tell about the last weeks of her last winter. They left her mark on them. They spoke of her, not knowing she had died. I didn't tell them. Nor that her name was Mona Bergeron. I know little about her myself, but it seems to me she came from the sea.

From there, the film jumps back in time, retracing Mona's (Sandrine Bonnaire) steps in the lead-up to her inevitable death. As Mona navigates a life without work, permanent shelter and, seemingly, without purpose, Varda introduces a series of characters, played by mostly non-professional actors from the region, who each describe their fleeting interactions with Mona. They occasionally speak directly to the camera as they attempt to assign meaning to her solitary existence. The film's original title, *Sans toit ni loi*, roughly translates to 'with neither roof nor law'. Taken as a whole, the phrase alludes to Mona's free-spirited, sometimes wild nature, but it also speaks to the fact that she exists outside of 'normal' society and is therefore vulnerable to those looking to take advantage of her vagrant lifestyle.

Shot in an unadorned *vérité* style, in washed-out tones that accentuate the bleakness of Mona's story, *Vagabond* appears at first glance to be a world away from the rigorous, highly stylized aesthetic of films like *The Grand Budapest Hotel* and *The French Dispatch* (2021). Dramatically speaking, it has little in common with Anderson's work; he has certainly never written a female protagonist as complex as Mona, or explored a character's life in such close, unflinching detail. Visually, Anderson's style is more consistent with Varda's earlier film *Le Bonheur* (*Happiness*, 1965). Yet there are several techniques that Varda employs in *Vagabond*, including flashbacks, fourth-wall breaking and voiceover narration, which have become Anderson hallmarks.

Anderson is particularly indebted to Varda's inventive use of lateral tracking shots. Mona is constantly on the move, her restlessness – and the film's fragmented structure – signified by the way the camera follows her from one place to the next. As she roams through barren fields and empty streets, she sometimes enters the frame while the camera is already in motion; at other times, it struggles to keep up and she walks right out of shot. Not only does this bring the viewer physically in step with Mona, but it also highlights the alienation and dislocation she feels. Anderson, of course, is no stranger to dolly shots; he uses one similarly to Varda in *Moonrise Kingdom* (2012) to bring Sam (Jared Gilman) and Suzy (Kara Hayward) together, and in *The Grand Budapest Hotel*, the camera moves with the unnamed girl as she walks through Old Lutz Cemetery, the rows of shabby, lopsided gravestones behind her adding to the sombreness of the scene.

In contrast to the dynamic tracking shots found in *Vagabond*, Varda includes numerous static close-ups of Mona's hands, usually on their own but sometimes shown next to another character's to further emphasize the squalid conditions she has exposed herself to. These intimate shots are primarily used to strengthen the connection between the viewer and the film's ill-fated heroine. Anderson also has a penchant for showing characters' hands up close. While this is typically from an overhead perspective rather than side on, as in *Vagabond*, the effect is the same: it links them in a physical, tactile way to an object or another character, and by extension the audience.

On a different note, there is an astonishing sequence in *Vagabond* where a middle-class academic named Madame Landier (Macha Méril), who is one of very few people in the film to show Mona genuine kindness and sympathy, and the only one to extract any information from her about her previous life as a secretary, is electrocuted in her home. We hear it first: a low, irregular rattle. Then we see Madame Landier's face reflected in her bathroom mirror – literally fixed in shock as she grips a faulty light fixture with both hands before eventually being freed by a colleague who has come to visit her.

It's conceivable that Madame Landier's brush with death – a freakish *deus ex machina* that causes her to re-evaluate her attitude towards Mona, as well as her own life – could have inspired the many electrified near misses in Anderson's films: Margot's (Gwyneth Paltrow) precariously poised bathtub television in *The Royal Tenenbaums*; Mr Fox (George Clooney) and Kylie's (Wallace Wolodarsky) high-voltage escape in *Fantastic Mr. Fox* (2009); the lightning strike that momentarily fells Sam in *Moonrise Kingdom*; and Moses Rosenthaler (Benicio Del Toro) strapping himself into an electric chair in *The French Dispatch*. Others, of course, aren't so lucky: Rat (Willem Dafoe) in *Fantastic Mr. Fox* and Zeffirelli (Timothée Chalamet) in *The French Dispatch* both meet a high-voltage end.

THERE ARE SEVERAL TECHNIQUES THAT VARDA EMPLOYS IN *VAGABOND*, INCLUDING FLASHBACKS, FOURTH-WALL BREAKING AND VOICEOVER NARRATION, WHICH HAVE BECOME ANDERSON HALLMARKS

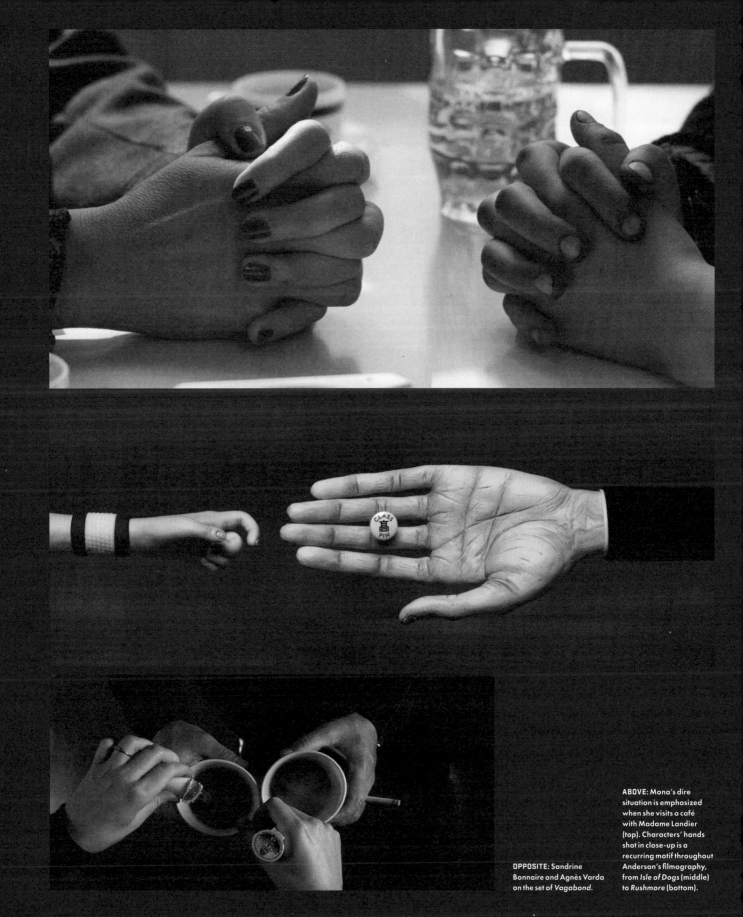

OPPOSITE: Sandrine Bonnaire and Agnès Varda on the set of *Vagabond*.

ABOVE: Mona's dire situation is emphasized when she visits a café with Madame Landier (top). Characters' hands shot in close-up is a recurring motif throughout Anderson's filmography, from *Isle of Dogs* (middle) to *Rushmore* (bottom).

'STOP BEING SO VIRTUOUS. I KNOW YOU'RE JUST OUT FOR YOURSELF.' – L'INSPECTEUR ADJOINT ANTOINE

OPPOSITE: An inspector calls: With his Charlie Chaplin moustache and general air of authority, L'inspecteur adjoint Antoine (top) provided Anderson with the perfect template for The Commissaire in *The French Dispatch* (bottom).

PART 3
Quai des Orfèvres

(*Goldsmiths' Quay*, Henri-Georges Clouzot, 1947)

Also on Anderson's *Sight and Sound* list was Henri-Georges Clouzot's *Quai des Orfèvres* (*Goldsmiths' Quay*), which explores the inner workings of a police investigation following a mysterious homicide; the title referring to the then-location of the Parisian headquarters of France's national police force. Loosely adapted from Belgian illustrator and author Stanislas-André Steeman's 1942 novel *Légitime Défense*, *Quai des Orfèvres* begins by teasing a *ménage à trois* between vivacious music hall singer Jenny Lamour (Suzy Delair), her jealous pianist husband Maurice (Bernard Blier) and a lecherous older man named Georges Brignon (Charles Dullin), who promises Jenny a plum role in a film he's financing.

Convinced that Jenny is carrying on behind his back, Maurice pays Brignon a visit one night with the intention of murdering him, only to discover that someone has beaten him to it. But who? Hot on the case is L'inspecteur adjoint Antoine (Louis Jouvet), a seasoned sleuth whose crime-solving skills and immaculately manicured facial hair would put Hercule Poirot to shame. In this thorny moral maze of a film, everyone is in a twist over Jenny, including Dora (Simone Renant), a studio photographer who lives downstairs from Maurice and Jenny, and who turns up at the scene of the crime to rid it of any evidence that might incriminate either of her friends. Dora is Antoine's first port of call, but it's not long before he turns his attention to her neighbours.

'The Private Dining Room of the Police Commissioner', the third and final story in *The French Dispatch*, was chiefly inspired by two autobiographical essays. The first was James Baldwin's 'Equal in Paris', originally published in *Commentary* magazine in 1955, in which, like the food journalist Roebuck Wright (Jeffrey Wright) in Anderson's movie, Baldwin describes being briefly detained in a police cell that resembles 'a chicken coop'. The other was A.J. Liebling's *New Yorker* article 'A Good Appetite', in which the writer invokes Marcel Proust while describing – at salivating length – his gastronomic exploits in the French capital in the late 1950s.

This section of *The French Dispatch* could best be described as a 'culinary noir'. The esteemed and enigmatic private chef at the centre of the story, Lieutenant Nescaffier (Stephen Park), was named after Georges Auguste Escoffier, who codified French cooking techniques in the early nineteenth century. The character was also partly based on the Japanese-French painter and printmaker Tsuguharu Foujita. But the procedural elements of 'The Private Dining Room of the Police Commissioner' are straight out of *Quai des Orfèvres*.

Anderson provided the cast and crew of *The French Dispatch* with a list of five films to watch ahead of production, one of which was *Quai des Orfèvres*; according to cinematographer Robert Yeoman, the other films on the list were Clouzot's *Les diaboliques* (*The Devils*, 1955), Max Ophüls' *Le plaisir* (*House of Pleasure*, 1952), Jean-Luc Godard's *Vivre sa vie* (*It's My Life*, 1962) and François Truffaut's *Les quatre cents coups* (*The 400 Blows*, 1959). The inclusion of *Quai des Orfèvres* would have been of particular interest to Mathieu Amalric, whose Commissaire, with his slicked back hair, Charlie Chaplin moustache, three-piece pinstripe suit and black polka dot bow tie, is a dead ringer for Jouvet's debonair, hawk-eyed investigator.

Beyond these superficial similarities, Anderson borrowed several backstory details from Clouzot and Jean Ferry's screenplay, such as Amalric's character having been a former Legionnaire and having an adopted son whom he brought back from an unspecified French colony. Considering Anderson's preoccupation with father–child relationships, it is not surprising that the Commissaire's son, Gigi (Winsen Ait Hellal, playing another of Anderson's prodigious pipsqueaks), is given a much bigger role than Antoine's. It is Gigi's kidnapping at the hands of a criminal gang led by Edward Norton's chauffeur that really gives Roebuck Wright something to sink his journalistic teeth into.

Both stories do, however, resolve themselves in the same way – not in a hail of bullets or with a chaotic car chase across town, but with a father sharing a light-hearted moment with his son. Upon being rescued, Gigi instinctively sucker punches his father square in the jaw, prompting the pair to break into relieved laughter. After Antoine solves Brignon's murder, his son playfully socks him with a snowball in front of Maurice and Jenny's apartment block, instantly dissolving the tension that has been gradually building throughout the film.

Clouzot could sometimes be heavy-handed in his directing style – quite literally in the case of *Quai des*

Orfèvres: he allegedly slapped Blier right before shooting the interrogation scene to elicit the desired look of shock from the actor – but he was undoubtedly a master when it came to creating realistic, lived-in worlds on screen. Anderson shares Clouzot's keen eye for staging. Like *Quai des Orfèvres*, *The French Dispatch*, particularly the final section, contains a colourful array of supporting characters – from hard-nosed cops and glassy-eyed showgirls to world-weary reporters and veteran concierges – who give the story an added layer of authenticity. Saoirse Ronan's junkie sex worker, who sings to Gigi the traditional French lullaby 'À la claire fontaine' (which is also sung in Louis Malle's 1987 film *Au revoir les enfants/Goodbye, Children*), looks like she has just stepped off a Clouzot set.

Although Clouzot's filmography mainly comprises tales of corruption, infidelity and murder, suggesting someone in possession of a rather cynical worldview, he preferred to let the viewer pass judgement on the actions and attitudes of his characters. He always took great care to humanize those deemed blameworthy in the eyes of the law or the court of public opinion. Consider the scene late on in *Quai des Orfèvres* where a tormented Maurice, having been formally charged with Brignon's murder, slashes his wrists with a piece of broken glass. The way Clouzot films this moment is deeply empathetic; the editing and sudden drop in sound reminiscent of Richie's (Luke Wilson) attempted suicide in *The Royal Tenenbaums*.

LEFT: The official French theatrical poster for *Quai des Orfèvres* (left).

Stephen Park's Lt. Nescaffier (middle) was partly based on the bohemian Japanese-French painter Tsuguharu Foujita (right).

OPPOSITE: A bust of *Tintin* creator Hergé stands in the centre of the French city of Angoulême.

CAPITAL OF CARTOONS

Towards the end of 'The Private Dining Room of the Police Commissioner', the story switches from live-action to a traditional hand-drawn cartoon animated in the style of two popular French-language comics: Edgar P. Jacobs' *Blake and Mortimer* and Hergé's *The Adventures of Tintin*. All the animation in *The French Dispatch* was directed by Gwenn Germain, who also worked on the 2D animated scenes in *Isle of Dogs*. Germain told *Animation Magazine* in 2021:

> The whole process of animation took about seven months. The challenge was to adapt and mix the two different references. [Anderson] has precise storyboards: he draws the backgrounds, and the actors are directed just like animated characters.

These animated sequences were produced in Angoulême, a small city in France where many of *The French Dispatch*'s live-action scenes were also filmed. Known as the 'Capital of Cartoons', Angoulême is home to the Festival International de la Bande Dessinée – the second largest comics festival in Europe – and la Cité, an arts centre, cinema and museum dedicated to archiving French and American comics. In the centre of Angoulême stands a bust of the Tintin creator, sculpted by the artist's good friend Chang Chong-jen, who was the inspiration for the Tintin story *The Blue Lotus*.

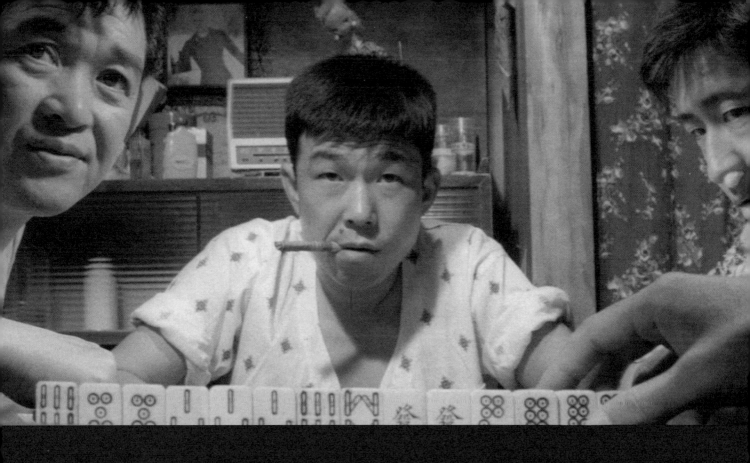

'I WANT TO DO SOMETHING COOL WITH MY LIFE. I WANT BETTER FOR MYSELF, AND FOR YOU TOO.' – KINTA

OPPOSITE: Centre
of attention: Central
framing is a key
aspect of Imamura's
filmmaking style (top),
and may have informed
Anderson's penchant for
compositional symmetry,
as demonstrated in *The
French Dispatch* when
Zeffirelli and his comrades
engage in a heated
political debate at Le Sans
Blague café (bottom).

PART 4
Pigs and Battleships

(Shôhei Imamura, 1961)

After Akira Kurosawa and Yasujirō Ozu, the Japanese filmmaker who has had the most pronounced influence on Anderson is Shôhei Imamura. When Anderson was asked by the *Criterion Collection* to name his top ten titles in their catalogue, he picked three films by Shôhei Imamura: *Pigs and Battleships, The Insect Woman* (1963) and *Intentions of Murder* (1964), while also mentioning another favourite, *Vengeance is Mine* (1979). Thematically and tonally, *Pigs and Battleships* feels the most Andersonian, so it merits closer inspection.

Set in the American-occupied port town of Yokosuka, Imamura's fifth feature follows Kinta (Hiroyuki Nagato), a lackey for the local *yakuza* (gangsters), and his girlfriend Haruko (Jitsuko Yoshimura), who works in a bar. Kinta's main gig is running the organization's lucrative pig farm, which supplies meat via the black market to sailors on shore leave and other non-Japanese interlopers. But he is constantly being roped into other, more seedy business matters. When the body of a rival gang leader washes up in the wharf, along with two drowned dogs, Kinta offers to take the fall in a bid to impress his bosses, much to the dismay of Haruko, who repeatedly tries and fails to persuade her lover to abandon his illicit lifestyle.

Once a quiet fishing village, Yokosuka is portrayed throughout the film as a den of vice. Its bustling, neon-soaked streets have something in common with the narrow, brightly lit back alleys of Megasaki City in *Isle of Dogs*, although Imamura's vision is much less romantic. At times, the place looks like a literal pigsty, with the presence of the US Navy and its fleets of hulking, sex-hungry GIs having corroded traditional Japanese culture. To all intents and purposes, *Pigs and Battleships* is a spiky post-war satire with a strong anti-imperialist message. But Imamura is also quick to show how his people – and not only those in positions of power or of a criminal persuasion – found ways to turn their exploitation to their advantage.

Imamura started out as an assistant director at Shochiku Studios in Ofuna, where he worked on three projects under Ozu: *Early Summer* (1951), *The Flavor of Green Tea over Rice* (1952) and *Tokyo Story* (1953). It is somewhat ironic, then, that his acerbic, unsentimental examinations of contemporary Japanese society earned him a reputation as the anti-Ozu. Yet it is Imamura's wry sense of humour and his idiosyncratic style that are most relevant to Anderson. In *Pigs and Battleships*, Imamura's sociopolitical concerns are wrapped up in a freewheeling plot that occasionally spills over into outright farce; it would make a great double feature with Hal Ashby's *The Last Detail* (1973).

In one scene, Kinta's boss Tetsuji (Tetsurō Tamba), believing that he has just three days to live, stumbles onto a railway line in a suicidal haze. When a passing train knocks him back to safety, the camera cuts to a wide shot, revealing a billboard that reads 'Nissan Life Insurance: Live Life with a Smile' – a sight gag that wouldn't seem out of place in an Anderson film. There is also a moment when Haruko is pressured by her mother and sister to sell her body in order to live a more comfortable life. As the women quarrel, Imamura shifts our attention to the next room, where Haruko's younger brother is reading aloud from a school textbook: 'Japan is a beautiful country with a unique culture, able to incorporate the finer practices and customs of other countries.' Again, this is the kind of droll juxtaposition we've come to expect from Anderson.

Later in the film, Imamura demonstrates his visual flair to even more striking and poignant effect. Although Haruko is desperate to leave Yokosuka and start a new life with Kinta, she continually finds herself being dragged into his sordid world. In the film's most devastating and technically impressive scene, a drunk Haruko is taken to a hotel room by three sailors and raped. Imamura spares the viewer the full horror of her ordeal. Instead, in a virtuosic move, he cuts to an aerial shot of the room and spins the camera rapidly, conveying at once Haruko's intoxicated state and the passing of time as night turns into day.

One function of the so-called God's-eye view shot, which is analyzed in greater detail in Chapter 8, is to encourage the viewer to consider an event from a moral standpoint. In this case, Imamura asks us to think about not just the rape, but also the wider subjugation of the Japanese people by the Allied powers, which continued long after the end of the Second World War. Anderson is one of modern cinema's most accomplished purveyors of this type of shot, and he learned from arguably the best to ever do it: Martin Scorsese. But if you want an even earlier example of a director expertly utilizing this technique, look no further than Imamura.

As in *Isle of Dogs*, the titular animals of *Pigs and Battleships* – not to mention Kinta, Haruko and the other lower-class citizens of Yokosuka – are depicted as pawns in a cruel game played by corrupt men. It is entirely apropos, then, that Kinta goes hog-wild at the end of the film, rebelling against his bosses by sabotaging a deal to sell off the gang's prized porcine stock. In a spectacular finale that

caused the production to go over budget, Kinta releases the pigs by the truckload while emptying a machine gun in the general direction of the mob, the police and anyone else who happens to be standing in his way.

Despite the high dramatic stakes of this scene, the frenzied pacing, coupled with Nagato's wonderfully clownish performance, gives it an almost slapstick feel. Long before directors such as Anderson and Scorsese were blending crime and violence with dark humour, Imamura delivered his own chaotic masterclass. He wasn't done there, though: the image of the liberated swines streaming through town, terrorizing locals and Americans alike, is followed by the arrival of yet more horny GIs, greeted off the boat by hordes of smiling Japanese women.

ABOVE: Imamura sees the funny side of a Tetsuji's near miss on a train track (top), while the aerial framing of Haruko's assault (bottom) may have inspired Anderson's signature use of the same technique.

OPPOSITE: The somewhat misleading poster for the US release of *Pigs and Battleships*.

TO ALL INTENTS AND PURPOSES, *PIGS AND BATTLESHIPS* IS A SPIKY POST-WAR SATIRE WITH A STRONG ANTI-IMPERIALIST MESSAGE

CHAPTER 8

CHARACTER AND PERSPECTIVE

'NO GUILT IS FORGOTTEN SO LONG AS THE CONSCIENCE STILL KNOWS OF IT.' – STEFAN ZWEIG, *BEWARE OF PITY*

OPPOSITE: A fitting
monument: The bronze
bust of Stefan Zweig in the
Jardin du Luxembourg,
Paris (top) resembles the
one of Tom Wilkinson's
Author seen at the start
of *The Grand Budapest
Hotel* (bottom).

PART 1
Stefan Zweig

Selected works

The Grand Budapest Hotel (2014) is Anderson's love letter to storytelling. The film is dedicated to Stefan Zweig, the Austrian Jewish writer who rose to fame in the 1920s before fleeing persecution from the Nazis in 1934. Despite being among the world's most translated authors at one time, Zweig's popularity has dwindled since his tragic suicide in 1942. Nevertheless, he was a bona fide celebrity in his day, regularly appearing on the radio, giving talks at prestigious universities and concert halls from London to New York, and even delivering a eulogy at the funeral of his close friend and compatriot, Sigmund Freud.

Anderson discovered Zweig completely by chance when he picked up a copy of his 1939 novel *Beware of Pity* at a second-hand bookshop in Paris. He became instantly obsessed, going so far as to use two of the author's best-known works as the basis for *The Grand Budapest Hotel*'s screenplay: the memoir *The World of Yesterday* and the novel *The Post Office Girl*, both published posthumously in 1942 and 1982, respectively. After its premiere at the 2014 Berlin International Film Festival, Anderson quipped that his film amounted to little more than plagiarism.

Zweig's books, many of which were banned and burned by the Nazis, are quite different in style and tone from Anderson's films, but *The Grand Budapest Hotel* explicitly joins the dots between their shared artistic sensibilities. For instance, Zweig's 1927 novella *24 Hours in the Life of a Woman* is written from the perspective of several narrators,

including a widowed English woman who recounts her scandalous, long-ago rendezvous with a caddish younger man at a Monte Carlo casino called the Grand Palace Hotel. The narrator in question is referred to simply as Mrs C.

Elsewhere, in *The Post Office Girl*, Zweig ruminates on the fractured and impoverished state of post-war Vienna through the melancholy tale of a postal clerk named Christine, who is left fatherless and penniless by the First World War. After accepting an invitation from a distant relative to vacation with them at a swanky resort in the Swiss Alps, Christine becomes enamoured with her new surroundings. Aided by her aunt, she attempts to conceal her low socioeconomic status by assuming the mores and mannerisms of the hotel's upper-class patrons. But her cover is blown, and she is forced to return home ignominiously.

In *Beware of Pity*, a cavalryman stationed on the Austro-Hungarian border in the lead-up to the First World War opens up to a writer about a shameful incident from his recent past. According to his story, the young officer is invited to dinner at the home of a local aristocrat, where he becomes infatuated with the man's attractive niece. As the evening draws to a close, our narrator finally plucks up the courage to ask the girl to dance, only to discover that she is unable to, having been paralyzed in a fall from a horse. Embarrassed, he runs away before eventually returning determined to improve the girl's situation. He extends her pity when all she really wants is his affection.

Any parallels between these stories and *The Grand Budapest Hotel* may seem purely cosmetic, but they all speak to Anderson's underlying fascination with characters reminiscing about their colourful, sometimes chequered pasts, be it to themselves, another character, or directly to the viewer. Moreover, the wistfulness with which the author-narrators of Zweig's work and Anderson's film discuss their youthful dalliances and indiscretions is laced with sadness and regret – the act of looking back invariably risks dredging up the memory of a doomed lover, a squandered opportunity or a tarnished reputation.

Beyond Zweig, *The Grand Budapest Hotel* is crammed with cinematic and literary allusions, all serving to remind the viewer that they have entered the realm of pure fiction – a story-within-a-story-within-a-story. The film's metatextual framework is established in its very first scene. A young woman steps into a cemetery in the old town of Lutz, located in the former Republic of Zubrowka 'on the farthest eastern boundary of the European continent' and which once was 'the seat of an Empire', as stated in a preceding title card, indicating a rich and complex history.

Before reaching the memorial in the middle of the cemetery, which structurally resembles the statue of Zweig located at the Jardin du Luxembourg in Paris, the woman passes three men dressed in black on a bench, singing a low choral chant. The men's shadowy presence instantly evokes that age-old paragon of literary symbolism, the three-pronged omen, most notably the Three Witches from Shakespeare's *Macbeth*. Their spectral appearance is mirrored later in the film in the form of Dmitri's (Adrien Brody) stern-faced sisters, who we first catch a glimpse of at the reading of Madame D.'s (Tilda Swinton) will.

Regarding the script's beginnings, Anderson revealed via the film's production notes:

I had an idea with my friend Hugo [Guinness]. He and I had talked for some years about a character inspired by a friend of ours, an exceptionally, supremely charming person with a unique and wonderful way with words and a very special view of life. Then, separately, I had this thought to make a kind of a European movie.

Into this mix, Anderson added several other accounts of how different nations responded to the rise of fascism, including Hannah Arendt's writings on the trial of Nazi war criminal Adolf Eichmann, collected as *Eichmann in Jerusalem: A Report on the Banality of Evil* (1963), and Irène Némirovsky's *Suite Française* (written 1942, published 2004).

Yet it is Zweig whose influence would prove to be the most significant. When M. Gustave (Ralph Fiennes) asks Zero (Tony Revolori) if he has ever been interrogated by the authorities, the trainee lobby boy reveals that he was once 'arrested and tortured by the rebel militia' in his unspecified country of origin following a period of civil unrest. Revolori's snappy delivery ensures that the line doesn't land too heavily, but the lasting impression is that of a courageous refugee whose young life has been marred by terrible events. Reflecting on his own time in exile, Zweig wrote in *The World of Yesterday*: 'Only the person who has experienced light and darkness, war and peace, rise and fall, only that person has truly experienced life.'

THE WISTFULNESS WITH WHICH THE AUTHOR-NARRATORS OF ZWEIG'S WORK AND ANDERSON'S FILM DISCUSS THEIR YOUTHFUL DALLIANCES AND INDISCRETIONS IS LACED WITH SADNESS AND REGRET

ABOVE: Henry Fuseli's 1783 painting *The Three Witches* depicting the ominous trio from Shakespeare's *Macbeth* (top), which are alluded to in the form of Dmitri's sisters, Marguerite, Laetizia and Carolina (middle).

RIGHT: The English-language cover of Zweig's 1942 memoir *The World of Yesterday: Memoires of a European* (left); the author working on his manuscripts, c. 1930 (right).

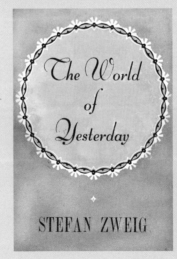

'BARRY WAS BORN CLEVER ENOUGH AT GAINING A FORTUNE,
BUT INCAPABLE OF KEEPING ONE.' – NARRATOR

OPPOSITE: Moonlight rendezvous: The scene where Barry makes his advances to Lady Lyndon (top) is recalled when Miss Cross reconciles with Herman during the intermission of Max's latest play in *Rushmore* (bottom).

PART 2
Barry Lyndon

(Stanley Kubrick, 1975)

At first glance, Anderson's work might not seem to have much in common with Stanley Kubrick's, but his filmography is loaded with call-backs to this undisputed master of cinema. Indeed, Anderson admitted in an interview with the *Hollywood Reporter* in 2012:

> Usually, by the time I'm making a movie, I don't really know where I'm stealing everything from. By the time it's a movie, I think, 'Oh, this is my thing', and I forget where I took it all – but I think I'm always pretty influenced by Kubrick.

In *The Grand Budapest Hotel*, the painting *Two Lesbians Masturbating*, which Zero replaces *Boy with Apple* with, was created by artist Rich Pellegrino in the style of Austrian painter Egon Schiele's erotic nudes, specifically *Two Girls, Lying Entwined* (1915) and *Reclining Woman* (1917) – yet it also recalls the graphic painting of a naked woman by pop artist Cornelius Makkink that hangs on the wall of Alex's bedroom in *A Clockwork Orange* (1971). The way M. Gustave and Zero run through the snow evokes Wendy (Shelley Duvall) and Danny's (Danny Lloyd) last-ditch escape from the Overlook Hotel in *The Shining* (1980). The masked animal figures that appear on the church balcony towards the end of *Moonrise Kingdom* (2012) are reminiscent of the cloaked sex cult in *Eyes Wide Shut* (1999). Jason Schwartzman's jaded photojournalist in *Asteroid City* (2023) is the spitting image of a young Kubrick, who worked

as a staff photographer at *Look* magazine before beginning his career in film. And the short film *Hotel Chevalier* (2007) takes its title from Patrick Magee's card-playing libertine in *Barry Lyndon*, the Chevalier de Balibari.

There are also similarities in how both directors utilize slow motion, dolly shots, crash zooms and whip pans. And there is one shot that has become as much a hallmark of Anderson's style as Kubrick's: one-point perspective. This simple but highly effective technique draws the viewer's focus towards a single vanishing point, usually in the dead centre of the frame. Although there is beauty in symmetry, we rarely see the world from this perspective, thus it can be disorienting for an audience. When used well, however, it can have a uniquely transfixing effect. Kubrick did not invent this technique; it has existed in art since at least the Italian Renaissance. But he arguably perfected it in a cinematic context. Indeed, every director that has come after Kubrick knowingly tips their hat to him whenever they use one-point perspective.

In *Barry Lyndon*, Kubrick employs an unconventional two-part structure, with intertitles announcing both distinct chapters, along with an intermission and an epilogue. He also uses an officious, omniscient narrator, voiced by Michael Hordern (who incidentally also narrated *Watership Down*, 1978). In doing so, Kubrick captures the epic sweep of a life that ultimately amounts to very little. Adapted from William Makepeace Thackeray's 1884 picaresque novel *The Luck of Barry Lyndon*, the film follows an opportunistic

ABOVE: Kubrick uses one-point perspective throughout *Barry Lyndon*, such as in the early battle scene (top left); Kubrick on the set of *Barry Lyndon* (top right).

Zero and M. Gustave running through a snowy field at dusk (bottom) evokes Wendy and Danny's final escape at the end of *The Shining* (middle).

ABOVE: Nods to Kubrick abound
in Anderson's work, with the
costumed children in *Moonrise
Kingdom* (top) resembling
masked figures in *Eyes Wide
Shut* (middle), and Max's
Vietnam War–themed
play (bottom right) calling
to mind *Full Metal Jacket*
(bottom left).

Irish rogue named Redmond Barry (Ryan O'Neal), who charms and chances his way across Europe during the Seven Years' War before settling in England with the Countess of Lyndon (Marisa Berenson), where he assumes her name, not to mention her many privileges. In charting the title character's heady rise and humiliating fall, Kubrick at once reveals his bone-dry sense of humour and his deep-lying fascination with some of the most pernicious human impulses – avarice, greed, jealousy, lust, spite.

Kubrick uses one-point perspective in *Barry Lyndon* for a few reasons. First, to highlight the picturesque landscapes of County Carlow and County Kildare in Ireland, where most of the early scenes were filmed; in terms of the composition and lighting of these exquisite exterior shots, Kubrick and cinematographer John Alcott took inspiration from oil paintings by period artists such as Thomas Gainsborough and John Constable. Second, to create dramatic tension, such as when Barry gets his first taste of battle and in the final, fateful duel between Barry and his resentful stepson Lord Bullingdon (Leon Vitali). And third, to call our attention to the opulent artifice of both the characters' surroundings and the film itself.

Anderson uses one-point perspective in a slightly different but equally striking way. Because this type of shot typically results in perfectly symmetrical composition, it might be assumed that Anderson favours it primarily for its aesthetic qualities. As the consummate, uncompromising formalist that he is, there is a perception of Anderson that he simply loves to flaunt his craft. Yet the geometric precision of his films has another function: to create order, however fleetingly, out of the chaos of his characters' lives. Where Kubrick tended to direct the viewer's gaze this way as a means of eliciting a sense of foreboding, Anderson does so in a more reassuring manner, continually re-centring our perspective to keep us grounded in the story while at the same time encouraging us to empathize with the characters. Although one-point perspective is considered unnaturalistic by many film theorists, Anderson conversely uses it to enhance the emotional realism of his work.

Beyond one-point perspective, Anderson further borrows from *Barry Lyndon* at the end of *Rushmore* (1998) during the intermission to Max's (Jason Schwartzman) play 'Heaven and Hell', which parodies several Vietnam War

movies, including Francis Ford Coppola's *Apocalypse Now* (1979), Brian De Palma's *Casualties of War* (1989), Oliver Stone's *Platoon* (1986) and *Heaven & Earth* (1993), and Kubrick's *Full Metal Jacket* (1987). When Miss Cross (Olivia Williams) steps outside the school hall, offering Herman (Bill Murray) a cup of coffee as an olive branch, the set-up is almost identical to the scene where Barry follows Lady Lyndon out onto a moonlit porch during a break in a card game, seizing the opportunity to make his move. Kubrick conveys this wordless eruption of emotion with a subtlety that betrays his genius, while Anderson demonstrates similar restraint to articulate a quiet moment of reconciliation where true feelings go unspoken. 'So, what do you think of Max's latest opus?' Miss Cross asks. 'It's good,' Herman replies. 'But let's hope it's got a happy ending.'

OPPOSITE: Gustav Klimt's *Adele Bloch-Bauer I* (1907; left) inspired some of Tilda Swinton's costumes in *The Grand Budapest Hotel* (right).

THE GEOMETRIC PRECISION OF [ANDERSON'S] FILMS HAS ANOTHER FUNCTION: TO CREATE ORDER, HOWEVER FLEETINGLY, OUT OF THE CHAOS OF HIS CHARACTERS' LIVES

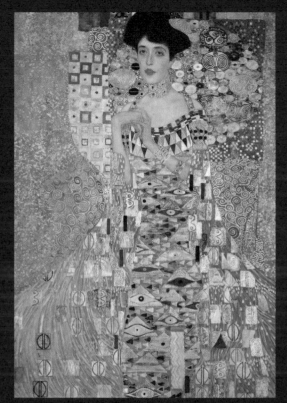

THE ART OF FASHION

With the exception of *Moonrise Kingdom*, Anderson has worked with the same costume designer on all of his live-action films since *The Life Aquatic with Steve Zissou* (2004): Milena Canonero. Born in Turin, Canonero studied art history and costume design in Genoa before moving to England, where she got her break in film with Stanley Kubrick's *A Clockwork Orange*. She designed the costumes for two more Kubrick films, *Barry Lyndon* and *The Shining*, winning the first of her four Academy Awards for the former. Her most recent Oscar came in 2015 for her work on *The Grand Budapest Hotel*.

During their long and fruitful creative partnership, Anderson and Canonero have collaborated with numerous high-end fashion designers: Marc Jacobs created the custom Louis Vuitton suitcases that appear in *The Darjeeling Limited* (2007), embellished with a wildlife pattern illustrated by Anderson's brother Chase; Fendi made Henckel's (Edward Norton) grey astrakhan coat and Madame D.'s mink-collared red velvet cape for *The Grand Budapest Hotel*, while Prada produced Jopling's (Willem Dafoe) leather trench coat for the same film. Canonero has also taken inspiration from the art world, referencing paintings by George Grosz, Gustav Klimt, Kees van Dongen and Tamara de Lempicka in her costume designs for several characters in *The Grand Budapest Hotel*.

'YOU DON'T MAKE UP FOR YOUR SINS IN THE CHURCH.
YOU DO IT IN THE STREETS.' – NARRATOR

OPPOSITE: Strike it lucky: The mercurial Johnny Boy lights a firecracker next to his long-suffering pal Charlie (top). Anderson pays homage to this scene in *Bottle Rocket* when Dignan buys a gun and lets off fireworks in a field (bottom).

PART 3
Mean Streets

(Martin Scorsese, 1973)

During a televised conversation with Roger Ebert, Martin Scorsese named *Bottle Rocket* (1996) as one of his ten favourite films of the 1990s. Later, in a piece for *Esquire* titled 'The Next Scorsese', the director heaped further praise on Anderson, writing of his heir apparent:

[He] has a very special kind of talent: He knows how to convey the simple joys and interactions between people so well and with such richness. This kind of sensibility is rare in movies . . . I remember seeing [Jean] Renoir's films as a child and immediately feeling connected to the characters through his love for them. It's the same with Anderson. I've found myself going back and watching *Bottle Rocket* several times . . . The central idea of the film is so delicate, so human: A group of young guys think that their lives have to be filled with risk and danger in order to be real. They don't know that it's okay simply to be who they are.

It's hardly surprising that Scorsese responded so strongly to Anderson's debut feature, given how clearly it echoes his own early work. Indeed, Anderson has cited *Mean Streets*, Scorsese's breakthrough, as a major influence on *Bottle Rocket* – not just for its catchy jukebox soundtrack, as mentioned in Chapter 1, but also for its use of a specific camera angle that is associated with both directors for different reasons: the God's-eye view shot. Although

conventionally used to establish a detached, neutral perspective, this technique – where the camera is placed directly above the subject, usually at a 90-degree angle so that it faces straight down – can also help to invest the viewer in a scene by allowing them to experience the action through a character's eyes.

The God's-eye view shot is aptly named in Scorsese's case. His strict Catholic upbringing instilled in him a faith that he has repeatedly contemplated and interrogated throughout his career. *Mean Streets*, *Taxi Driver* (1976), *Raging Bull* (1980) and *Goodfellas* (1990) all centre on tormented male protagonists who observe certain religious rituals while at the same time committing violent criminal acts. By invoking God's perspective, Scorsese actively engages the audience in the complex, sometimes ambiguous, morality of his characters. He invites us not necessarily to pass judgement but simply to consider them from an elevated vantage point. In Scorsese's films, this type of shot typically has a symbolic function as well as a practical one.

Like Scorsese, Anderson employs God's-eye view in a compelling, highly personal way. He often uses it for close-up insert shots, cutting from a medium or wide shot to highlight not just an action but a particular object, such as a stylus being carefully dropped onto a record (in *The Royal Tenenbaums*, 2001) or prisoners' hands grabbing hungrily at a freshly sliced Mendl's cake (in *The Grand Budapest Hotel*). As noted by Luís Azevedo in his video essay on Anderson's use of God's-eye view, he has a habit of shooting literary objects from above: 'Lists, novels, ransom notes, newspapers, posters, letters. . .' This can be expanded to include just about every kind of printed material: business cards, certificates, maps, menus, postcards, identification papers, escape plans, song sheets, telegrams, travel brochures, and so on. In an Anderson film, any given object might serve as a plot point or contain a crucial piece of information about a character. In short, they always tell a story.

Bottle Rocket features one of Anderson's signature overhead shots. During the diner scene, the camera switches to a top-down point of view just as Anthony (Luke Wilson) spins a piece of paper around to show Dignan (Owen Wilson) – and the viewer – a drawing of his new crush, Inez (Lumi Cavazos). The amusingly crude crayon sketch reinforces Anthony's childlike innocence, which is gradually eroded over the course of the film. In *Mean Streets*, Robert De Niro's Johnny Boy, whose very name implies a basic lack of maturity, is portrayed as similarly naive, although his put-on bravado and reckless behaviour are more reminiscent of Dignan than Anthony. 'Watch this, I'm gonna shoot the light out of the Empire State Building,' Johnny Boy shouts as he empties his .38 into the night sky from the top of a tenement building – a line that, in a different context, wouldn't seem out of place coming from Owen Wilson's wannabe anti-hero.

Another technique favoured by both Anderson and Scorsese is slow motion. Although commonplace today,

slow motion didn't enter the lexicon of mainstream American cinema until the late 1960s, when Arthur Penn and Sam Peckinpah used it in the bloody climaxes of *Bonnie and Clyde* (1967) and *The Wild Bunch* (1969), respectively. Each director was in his own way paying tribute to Akira Kurosawa, who utilized slow motion to similarly powerful effect in *Seven Samurai* (1954) a decade earlier, giving the now-iconic sword fight scenes added dramatic thrust. Kurosawa inspired a whole generation of Hollywood filmmakers, including Scorsese, who more than any of his contemporaries would go on to make this technique his own.

Rather than drawing out a moment of shocking violence, Scorsese uses slow motion in *Mean Streets* to accentuate a character's mood. When Johnny Boy strides confidently through a dimly lit nightclub, a broad grin on his face and a girl under each arm, his friend and protector Charlie (Harvey Keitel) watches him with wary intent. Anderson and his longtime cinematographer, Robert Yeoman, have matched the set-up of this shot on multiple occasions, most memorably when Margot Tenenbaum (Gwyneth Paltrow) steps off the Green Line bus and glides towards Richie (Luke Wilson), who is sitting waiting for her, having just returned from his solo round-the-world cruise. The scene is primarily framed from Richie's perspective, the way the camera lingers on Margot's face suggesting a love so great that time itself seems to slow down for it.

FAR LEFT: Robert De Niro, Martin Scorsese and Harvey Keitel on the set of *Mean Streets*.

LEFT: The official US theatrical poster for the film.

ABOVE: God's-eye view shots feature heavily in both Scorsese's and Anderson's films, from Travis purchasing a handgun in *Taxi Driver* (top), to Anthony revealing his romantic doodle to Dignan in *Bottle Rocket* (middle), to Madame D.'s open casket in *The Grand Budapest Hotel* (bottom left), and Tommy getting whacked in *Goodfellas* (bottom right).

'A DANCER WHO RELIES UPON THE DOUBTFUL COMFORTS OF HUMAN LOVE CAN NEVER BE A GREAT DANCER. NEVER.' – BORIS LERMONTOV

OPPOSITE: By the book:
The Red Shoes' title
sequence features a gently
flickering candle (top), an
image which Anderson
doubles up on at the start
of *The Royal Tenenbaums*
(bottom).

PART 4
The Red Shoes

(Michael Powell, Emeric Pressburger, 1948)

Under the banner of 'The Archers', Michael Powell and Emeric Pressburger collaborated 17 times between 1939 and 1957, a creative partnership that produced some of the most innovative and original films of British cinema's first golden age. While promoting *Moonrise Kingdom* in 2012, Anderson said of the pair's influence on his work:

> For many years some of the movies that have most inspired me, especially in a visual way, are the Michael Powell and Emeric Pressburger films [. . .] So much of that work is about making these visual. . . quite artificial films, and there's something very exciting about what they've made that's in front of the camera [. . .] You really are transported to that place, but you feel that someone has made these things and they're very emotional, moving films.

It is more than likely that Anderson gave the Tenenbaums the fictional street address 111 Archer Avenue as an homage to the British filmmaking duo. Indeed, at the beginning of the director's commentary for *The Royal Tenenbaums*, Anderson states that 'one of the initial ideas for this movie was that it would be based on a book – a book that doesn't actually exist'. He goes on to explain that the film's title sequence was directly inspired by Powell and Pressburger, 'especially *The Red Shoes*'.

Adapted from Hans Christian Andersen's classic fairy tale of the same name, *The Red Shoes* is a swooning melodrama about an obsessive, prodigiously talented ballerina named Victoria Page (Moira Shearer, miraculous in her big-screen debut). After joining a world-famous ballet company run by the brilliant but demanding impresario Boris Lermontov (Anton Walbrook), she falls in love with an up-and-coming composer named Julian Craster (Marius Goring) and is forced to choose between following her dreams or her heart. For Victoria, dancing literally becomes a matter of life and death.

Embracing its literary origins, *The Red Shoes* opens in time-honoured storybook fashion. The camera pulls back from a close-up of a lit candle to reveal the film's title written in what appears to be lipstick – or is it blood? – on a scorched piece of parchment. In the foreground, the eponymous red pumps rest next to a leather-bound volume of Andersen's fairy tales. The whole image has a painterly appearance; were it not for the gentle flicker of the candle's flame, it could easily be mistaken for an actual still life. Everything from the production and set design to the costumes, choreography and music is designed to pull the audience further into the enchanted world of the film. But it is the title sequence that immediately establishes the film's imagined perspective.

As previously discussed, this self-reflexive framing device is a recurring motif in Anderson's work. Many of his films are imbued with a sense of heightened reality that stems from his fondness of frame stories. *Rushmore*, *The Royal Tenenbaums*, *The Life Aquatic with Steve Zissou*, *The Darjeeling Limited*, *Moonrise Kingdom*, *The Grand Budapest Hotel*, *The French Dispatch* (2021) and *Asteroid City* all contain stories within the main narrative that are authored by one or several of the main characters, be it in the form of a play, a novel, a documentary, a journal, a memoir or a magazine article; sometimes, their introduction is signalled by a shift in aspect ratio. A few of Anderson's films use the exact same framing device as *The Red Shoes* – the library book shown at the start of *The Royal Tenenbaums* even features a pair of candles on its cover.

In his autobiography, *A Life in Movies*, Powell wrote that the point of the film's tragic ending was to highlight 'the conflict between romance and realism, between theatre and life'. A similar conflict exists in Anderson's work. His highly stylized, hermetically sealed worlds may seem a tad stagey at times, bordering on the surreal at others, but through them he explores universal themes in a way that always feels relatable and never overly contrived. He creates dazzling snow globes in which audiences can see their own lives reflected.

Another aspect of *The Red Shoes* that has provided inspiration for Anderson is its ravishing colour palette. The film was lensed by legendary cinematographer Jack Cardiff using three-strip Technicolor, a complex process that produced unrivalled images, but which was also extremely expensive; by the mid-1950s, it had been supplanted by cheaper, simpler methods. *The Red Shoes* has long been considered the gold standard of this now obsolete technique – none other than Natalie Kalmus, who was married to Technicolor pioneer Herbert Kalmus and was credited as colour consultant on every major Technicolor film between 1934 and 1949, thought it the greatest colour film ever made.

Anderson's own use of colour is no less distinctive. Picture any of his films and certain shades will no doubt spring to mind, from the primary colours of *The Life Aquatic with Steve Zissou* to the earthy hues of *Fantastic Mr. Fox* (2009) to the soft pastels of *The Grand Budapest Hotel*. *The Red Shoes* is a film about intense passions, and without wishing to dive too deep into colour theory at this stage, its vivid aesthetic casts an irresistible spell, not only helping to transport the viewer but also eliciting the same emotions as those experienced by the lead characters. The next time you watch an Anderson film, think about the colours he uses and how they make you feel (more on this in the next chapter).

Anderson has also acknowledged the influence of Powell and Pressberger's use of music, specifically on *Moonrise Kingdom*:

The Red Shoes is a movie where there's a very long sequence where the music was written first and the movie was made to the music . . . In our movie this Benjamin Britten music that we use – a lot of the movie was choreographed to it, and we drew a lot of the scenes and semi-animated them in advance. So we sort of knew where the cuts were going to be based on the music.

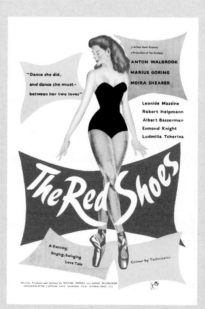

LEFT: The official US theatrical poster for *The Red Shoes*.

OPPOSITE: MTC driver Angela 'Johnny' Cannon, played by Deborah Kerr in *The Life and Death of Colonel Blimp* (top left), inspired the look of Social Services in *Moonrise Kingdom* (top right). In the same film, pilot Jed (bottom left) bears an uncanny resemblance to David Niven's RAF Squadron Leader Peter Carter in *A Matter of Life and Death* (bottom right).

FROM HEAVEN TO THE HIMALAYAS

Anderson's admiration for Powell and Pressburger extends far beyond *The Red Shoes*. In *Moonrise Kingdom*, Tilda Swinton's Social Services is styled to look like Deborah Kerr's various characters in *The Life and Death of Colonel Blimp* (1943), particularly the title character's personal army driver, Angela 'Johnny' Cannon. Swinton's character also has a brief exchange with a pilot who bears a certain resemblance to David Niven's RAF Squadron Leader in *A Matter of Life and Death* (1946), also known as *Stairway to Heaven*. In *The Grand Budapest Hotel*, Mr Moustafa (F. Murray Abraham) paraphrases a famous line from *The Life and Death of Colonel Blimp* when he narrates that 'the war began at midnight'.

'There's something very exciting about what [Powell and Pressburger] made in front of the camera,' Anderson told the *Washington Post* in 2012. Referring to *Black Narcissus* (1947), which is set in the Himalayas but was mostly filmed at Pinewood Studios in England, Anderson said: 'You were really transported to that place, but you [also felt] someone had made these things. And they're very emotional, moving films.' Inspired by *Black Narcissus*, Anderson set part of *The Darjeeling Limited* in a remote mountaintop convent in the Himalayas, where the Whitman brothers track down their mother Patricia. The establishing helicopter shot is of the Roothi Rani ka Mahal, a seventeenth-century palace near Udaipur in northern India.

CHAPTER 9

COLOUR AND COMPOSITION

'BECAUSE THE WORLD IS SO FAITHLESS, I GO MY WAY IN MOURNING.' – PIETER BRUEGEL THE ELDER

OPPOSITE: Setting the scene: Pieter Bruegel the Elder's 1565 painting *The Hunters in the Snow* captures an everyday scene of pastoral life in the sixteenthth century (top). *The Grand Budapest Hotel* contains a few subtle allusions to the painting, such as the shot of a bridge over a frozen river (bottom).

PART 1
Pieter Bruegel the Elder

Selected works

Art has always played a significant role in Anderson's work. His characters are sometimes amateur painters, such as Richie Tenenbaum (Luke Wilson) in *The Royal Tenenbaums* (2001), Mrs Fox (Meryl Streep) in *Fantastic Mr. Fox* (2009) and Sam Shakusky (Jared Gilman) in *Moonrise Kingdom* (2012). One is even a fully fledged virtuoso. 'The Concrete Masterpiece' story in *The French Dispatch* (2021) centres on the creation of an epic load-bearing fresco by incarcerated artist Moses Rosenthaler, played in turn by Benicio del Toro and Tony Revolori, which was painted for the film by German-New Zealand visual artist Sandro Kopp, assisted by Sian Smith and Edith Baudraud. For the other paintings featured in this part of the film – Rosenthaler's early works – Kopp and his team looked to the Swiss-French painter Félix Vallotton for inspiration.

In addition to the real – that is, pre-existing – paintings already mentioned in this book, numerous others appear as set dressing in several Anderson films. In *The Royal Tenenbaums*, Eli Cash (Owen Wilson) has two large canvases by Mexican artist Miguel Calderón in his apartment (both of which feature masked characters whose frightening appearance is evoked by the face paint Cash wears at the end of the film). Elsewhere, Anderson chose the Teatro di San Carlo in Naples as one of

the locations for *The Life Aquatic with Steve Zissou* (2004), in part because of its spectacular painted stage curtain by Giuseppe Mancinelli.

The Grand Budapest boasts a small but impressive Gustav Klimt collection, including *Avenue of Schloss Kammer Park* (1912); it's no coincidence that Ralph Fiennes' character M. Gustave shares a name with the Austrian painter. The large-scale scenic mural that adorns the hotel's dining room was created by artist Michael Lenz in the style of German painter Caspar David Friedrich, while the matte backdrops used throughout *The Grand Budapest Hotel* (2014) were made by Simone De Salvatore, some taking as long as three weeks to complete. There are also numerous shots in the film where the action is framed within a frame, giving the impression of a painting.

Regarding *The Grand Budapest Hotel*'s central plot device, the inheritance of the painting *Boy with Apple*, Anderson told the *Wall Street Journal* in 2014 that Agnolo Bronzino's portrait of the Florentine aristocrat Lodovico Capponi was a key reference, but that 'we were trying to suggest that it wasn't an Italian Renaissance painting. That it was more Northern [Renaissance].' In the same interview, Anderson namechecked Hans Holbein (although it is unclear whether he was referring to the Elder or the Younger) and Pieter Bruegel the Elder, one of the leading figures of the Dutch and Flemish Renaissance movement.

Four years after the making of *The Grand Budapest Hotel*, the Kunsthistorisches Museum in Vienna hosted an exhibition curated by Anderson and his partner, the writer and illustrator Juman Malouf. Among the 430 or so pieces the couple hand-picked from the museum's archives was Bruegel's famous painting *The Tower of Babel* (1563), which the artist based on the story from the book of Genesis in the Bible about a group of people who are punished by God for the sacrilegious act of attempting to build a city and a tower 'with its top in the heavens'.

Bruegel painted three versions of *The Tower of Babel*, each depicting the construction of the parabolic edifice,

and Anderson and Malouf chose the second for inclusion in their exhibition. Anderson being a great lover of imposing, intricately designed buildings, it's easy to see why Bruegel's masterpiece caught his eye – after all, what is the Grand Budapest if not an ornate monument to humanity's hubris and overambition, perched on a mountaintop reaching proudly up to the sky?

The tower may be the main focal point of Bruegel's painting, but if you study the image more closely, you will start to notice snapshots of everyday life dotted around the base of the structure, such as farmers making hay and two men unloading supplies from a small boat. These micro-scenes are rendered with the same level of care and precision as the tower, and as such they lend a sense of realism to what is otherwise an otherworldly artwork.

LEFT: The biblical Tower of Babel was the subject of three paintings by Bruegel; this 1563 version was featured in a 2014 exhibition curated by Anderson and Juman Malouf.

OPPOSITE: Replicas of several paintings by Gustav Klimt appear in *The Grand Budapest Hotel*, including 1912's *Avenue of Schloss Kammer Park* (top), which can be seen on the wall behind M. Gustave early in the film (bottom).

WHAT IS THE GRAND BUDAPEST IF NOT AN ORNATE MONUMENT TO HUMANITY'S HUBRIS AND OVERAMBITION?

Similarly, Anderson never overlooks the little things. As Sophie Monks Kaufman observes in her book *Close-Ups: Wes Anderson*, 'everything you can see [in the background of Anderson's frame] has a backstory'. In this sense, Anderson's work is reminiscent of another famous Bruegel painting housed at the Kunsthistorisches Museum, *Hunters in the Snow* (1565). In this wintry scene, three weary-looking hunters trudge home through the snow, shadowed by a pack of sad dogs. To their left, a group of villagers tend to a fire outside an inn, while in the valley beyond, others ice skate and play games on a frozen lake. In the far distance, a range of jagged peaks loom threateningly.

Although no individual frame in Anderson's oeuvre quite matches the dramatic composition of *Hunters in the Snow*, his use of colour and light, as well as the attention he gives to minor characters and small details, all evoke Bruegel's holistic approach to scene building. One of the best examples of this occurs at the beginning of *The French Dispatch*. Our first glimpse of the town Ennui-sur-Blasé reveals the offices of the eponymous publication. But this is no ordinary establishing shot. Below, an old man inspects a street map; a middle-aged woman waits to cross the street with her Dachshund; a deliveryman bundles stacks of magazines into the back of a van; a driving school car speeds past; a pair of police officers cycle in the opposite direction; a man smokes a cigarette outside a café; another man smokes a pipe; someone scoots by on a moped; a woman stands at her balcony sipping her morning coffee; a different dog trundles across the frame.

None of this is trivial. In the space of a few seconds, Anderson fully immerses the viewer in the world of the film; every aspect of this brief expositional scene is essential to our understanding of where and when the story is about to take place. A similar, still more characterful sequence occurs soon after in the travel guide section presented by 'Cycling Reporter' Herbsaint Sazerac (Owen Wilson), bringing us further in sync with Ennui's particular rhythms. As with Bruegel's captivating scenes of ordinary provincial life, as well as his more grandiose work, in Anderson's films there is always something to look at.

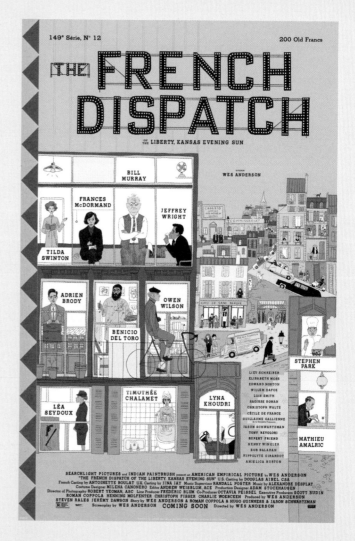

ABOVE: *The French Dispatch* film poster by illustrator Javi Aznarez, who also created *New Yorker*-style fictional magazine covers for Anderson's film.

OPPOSITE: Installation view of MoMA's 1965 exhibition *The Responsive Eye*.

THE RESPONSIVE EYE

In the spring of 1965, New York's Museum of Modern Art hosted an exhibition titled *The Responsive Eye*, which comprised over 120 pieces by up-and-coming avant-garde artists such as Bridget Riley, Jeffrey Steele and Larry Poons. The opening night was documented by a then-unknown American filmmaker named Brian De Palma. The resulting 25-minute short is part guided tour, part piss-take, with curator William C. Seitz and psychologist Rudolf Arnheim offering over-earnest appraisals of some of the cutting-edge op art on show, and various artists and pseudo-intellectuals making pithy offhand remarks to the camera.

In the end credits of *The French Dispatch*, Anderson gives special thanks to De Palma, and in the published edition of the film's screenplay, he explains that *The Responsive Eye* was the reason for this. At the same time, he cites Emile de Antonio's 1972 documentary *Painters Painting* as one of the inspirations for 'The Concrete Masterpiece'. According to Anderson, this definitive portrait of New York's art scene in the mid-twentieth century 'suggested to me the idea to shoot only the paintings in colour. Because [de Antonio] did that. I think, in his case, it might have been to save money on film stock for the interview parts of his film – but it is a beautiful effect.'

'THERE IS NO SUCH THING AS GOOD PAINTING
ABOUT NOTHING.' – MARK ROTHKO

OPPOSITE: The abstract truth: Mark Rothko's bold use of colour in paintings such as *Untitled* (1960; top left) and *Untitled* (1970; top right) have clearly had a major impact on Anderson's style, as evidenced in the Grand Budapest's red lift and purple staff uniforms (bottom).

PART 2
Mark Rothko

Selected works

While still living in Houston, Anderson was a regular visitor to the Rothko Chapel. This non-denominational spiritual space and modern art gallery was founded by philanthropist art collectors John and Dominique de Menil, who named it after the Latvian-born American artist Mark Rothko. In the early 1990s, Anderson attended a full retrospective of Rothko's work at the chapel, later recalling the transformative experience in a 2021 interview with the Houston-based news site Chron.com: 'Only in seeing the entire course of his work did I sort of get it. I saw something take shape in his thinking that was so interesting to me and that never left my mind.'

Rothko was the leading exponent of a subset of Abstract Expressionism known as colour-field painting, whereby artists saturated their canvases with large expanses of colour to fix the observer in an introspective state. As Rothko once put it, 'If you are only moved by colour relationships, you are missing the point. I am interested in expressing the big emotions – tragedy, ecstasy, doom, and so on.' In her video essay on references in Anderson's work, Candice Drouet places Rothko's *Orange and Yellow* (1956) alongside a picture of a sunset from *Fantastic Mr. Fox*, highlighting the warm autumnal hues of both images. Yet there are further shades of Rothko to be found in Anderson's filmography.

In *The Royal Tenenbaums*, the shot of a young Margot (Irene Gorovaia) and Chas (Aram Aslanian-Persico) leaning out of adjoining windows has the same tonal quality as several paintings by Rothko. As do the regal plum uniforms worn by the Grand Budapest's staff, the hotel's crimson-lacquered elevator (a blood-red lift is also always an allusion to Stanley Kubrick's *The Shining*, 1980) and the pink-and-blue branding of Mendl's patisserie. More specifically, there is an establishing shot in *The Grand Budapest Hotel* that recalls Rothko's *Blue, Green and Brown* (1952), with a snow-dusted pine forest fading into the distance behind the hotel until it meets a swirling midnight blue sky. In *Asteroid City* (2023), the horizon line often runs straight across the middle of the frame, the cerulean sky and ochre sand of the film's Southwest American setting creating a clean Rothko-esque contrast.

At the end of the 1940s, Rothko broke away from the more Surrealist-inspired paintings of his formative years and developed what is now regarded as his signature style. He achieved this by dividing the canvas horizontally into irregular rectangles of colour, which he then subtly blended into each other. One of his best-known pieces from this period, simply titled *No. 10* (1950), features a bold combination of blues and yellows that shows up everywhere in Anderson's work, namely in Team Zissou's crew uniform, diving gear and research submarine, the brightly painted carriages of the Darjeeling Limited, and the facade of *The French Dispatch*'s Le Sans Blague café.

There are also hints of Rothko's early work in Anderson's films. For instance, the thin, faceless figures of *Entrance to Subway* (1938) would not look out of place wandering the lobby of the Grand Budapest; both the film and the painting conjure similar feelings of isolation and loneliness. Whenever Anderson makes a film, he develops a distinctive colour palette that corresponds to the emotions of the characters and the themes of the story he is telling. Rothko's ideas about how different colours affect people's moods are infused into each and every one. Another painting from Rothko's unofficial subway series, *Untitled* (1936), depicts an anxious-looking woman in a red outfit standing alone on a platform, who bears a passing resemblance to Suzy Bishop (Kara Hayward, *Moonrise Kingdom*), Margot Tenenbaum (Gwyneth Paltrow, *The Royal Tenenbaums*) and Lucinda Krementz (Frances McDormand, *The French Dispatch*) rolled into one.

Red is perhaps the most prevalent colour in the work of both Anderson and Rothko. In Anderson's case, it often symbolizes trauma, as with Max's beret (Jason Schwarzman, *Rushmore*, 1998), Chas's tracksuit (Ben Stiller, *The Royal Tenenbaums*) and the vintage Porsche the Whitman brothers take to their father's funeral (*The Darjeeling Limited*, 2007). For Rothko, red also had great personal significance. As his physical and mental health deteriorated with age, blushed corals and candied reds gave way to deep maroons and dusky browns; the 14 paintings on permanent display at the Rothko Chapel, created between 1964 and 1967, are among the artist's darkest works, literally and figuratively. Like Rothko's paintings, Anderson's films, whether they are brightly or darkly coloured, invariably express big emotions — tragedy, ecstasy, doom, and everything in between.

Another important twentieth-century American painter who may have influenced Anderson is Milton Avery. A friend and mentor of Rothko, who considered Avery 'a great poet' first and foremost, Avery was renowned for his formally innovative portraits, landscapes and still lives, which typically reduced the artist's chosen subject to its most essential form through a combination of dense, flattened colours and soft, asymmetrical shapes. His seascape *Little Fox River* (1942) has something in common with Sam's painting of his and Suzy's sandy refuge in *Moonrise Kingdom*, while the more abstract *Boathouse by the Sea*

(1959) uses a deceptively simple palette that is at times echoed in the same film.

Returning to Houston, the Menil Collection, again founded by the eponymous couple, contains nearly 17,000 paintings, sculptures, prints, drawings, photographs and rare books, including multiple works by Andy Warhol, Bruce Davidson, Dorothea Tanning, Jasper Johns, Pablo Picasso, René Magritte, Joan Miró and, naturally, Rothko. Reflecting on the collection's influence on his own artistic development, Anderson told the *Houston Chronicle* in 2022:

For me, the Menil was like a magnificent teacher who you become friends with. I remember specific retrospectives: Robert Rauschenberg, John Chamberlain, Dan Flavin, Jean Tinguely, Edward Kienholz. Not just the work, but the evolution of the work — right there on the walls and floors . . . It will always be my favourite museum in the world.

THE THIN, FACELESS FIGURES OF *ENTRANCE TO SUBWAY* WOULD NOT LOOK OUT OF PLACE WANDERING THE LOBBY OF THE GRAND BUDAPEST

ABOVE: Further shades of
Rothko appear throughout
Anderson's filmography,
with Team Zissou's diving
gear and submersible (top
left) and the Darjeeling
Limited's painted
carriages (bottom left)
matching the bright hues
of Rothko's *Yellow, White,
Blue Over Yellow on Gray*
(1954; right).

RIGHT: The figure
disappearing down the
stairwell in Rothko's
slightly eerie 1938
painting *Entrance to
Subway* could be mistaken
for Zero from *The Grand
Budapest Hotel*, with the
grey-clad group in the
background resembling
a ZZ squad.

'PHOTOGRAPHY TO ME IS CATCHING A MOMENT WHICH IS PASSING, AND WHICH IS TRUE.' – JACQUES HENRI LARTIGUE

OPPOSITE: Picture perfect:
Jacques-Henri Lartigue's
1919 self-portrait, taken
at Cap du Dramont in
southern France (top),
appears in *The Life
Aquatic with Steve Zissou*
in the form of a painted
reproduction, with the
subject referred to as
Zissou's dead mentor
Lord Mandrake (bottom).

PART 3
Jacques Henri Lartigue

Selected works

Jacques Henri Lartigue looms large over Anderson's filmography. In *The Life Aquatic with Steve Zissou*, a painting of the French photographer, referred to as Zissou's dead mentor, Lord Mandrake, is seen hanging in the Explorers Club; the self-portrait it was based on appears later in the film during the boat tour sequence. In *Rushmore*, the brief shot of Max posing on a go-kart during the yearbook montage is a recreation of one of Lartigue's most famous photographs; earlier in the film the same image, along with three more by Lartigue, is shown pinned to the wall of Max's classroom. Lartigue's name is listed in the end credits for both films.

The subject of the latter photograph is Lartigue's older brother Maurice, known to his friends as 'Zissou'; the original title is 'Le bobsleigh à roues de Zissou, après le virage de la grille', or 'Zissou's bobsled with wheels, after the bend by the gate'. Acknowledging Lartigue's influence, Anderson wrote in the production notes for *Rushmore*: 'We looked at some pictures by Lartigue, who reminds me of Max.' In a 2005 interview with *AlloCiné*, the director added: '[Maurice] was in the pictures a lot, and he was absolutely brilliant. He did loads of stunts; he was a complete daredevil. I wanted to pay homage to him, even if the character of Zissou in the film is not really a daredevil.'

Despite being among the most celebrated photographers of the twentieth century, Lartigue did not receive international recognition until MoMA hosted a solo exhibition of his work in 1963, by which point he was 69. He was introduced to photography as a child more than half a century earlier: according to Lartigue's official website:

. . . his father gave him his first camera in 1902. From then on, Jacques recorded incessantly the world of his childhood . . . Born into a prosperous family, [Jacques and Maurice] were fascinated by cars, aviation and sports currently in vogue; Jacques used his camera to document them all.

All four photographs displayed behind Max in *Rushmore* depict such scenes. Aside from Maurice sitting on his bobsled, there is the moment he takes flight on a hand-built glider named 'ZYX 24' (implying a string of unsuccessful previous attempts); a Delage race car going flat out at the 1912 Grand Prix de l'Automobile Club de France, the vehicle's fierce velocity denoted by the diagonal onlookers and a distorted rear wheel; and a smartly dressed Maurice floating in a 'tire boat' of his own design, his legs submerged in the water inside a pair of rubber slacks attached to the vessel.

Aside from the fact that he mostly shot in black-and-white, Lartigue was highly unorthodox in his approach to chronicling the everyday lives and leisure activities of the French upper-middle classes. He was chiefly concerned with capturing a sense of freedom in his images, ignoring the rules of formal photography to achieve a naturalistic effect. As a result, his compositions were rarely staged. He often used dynamic angles to emphasize movement, and he employed a shallow depth of field to focus attention on a specific subject while allowing the background to blur or fade away, as in the Grand Prix image.

Lartigue's action-filled, apparently spontaneous photographs are at once exhilarating, surprising and mesmerizing. It's no wonder Anderson is such a fan. The 126 albums that make up his archives, currently housed at the Médiathèque du patrimoine et de la photographie on the outskirts of Paris, are not only an extraordinary 'visual diary' of an artist's 'personal and professional experiences', but they also provide a vital window to the past. At the same time, there is something thrillingly modern about Lartigue's work. Although the clothing, equipment and technology depicted in his photographs has changed over the years, the simple *joie de vivre* expressed by his subjects makes them instantly relatable and less old-fashioned than they might otherwise appear.

People seemingly defying or surrendering to gravity is a common theme. As is people pushing themselves or their various contraptions to the limits of performance. Although Anderson deals in moving pictures, pluck certain still frames from any of his films and you will find the same fluid motion and adrenalizing energy. Picture Steve Zissou (Bill Murray) cycling along the beach with his faithful crew running beside him (*The Life Aquatic with Steve Zissou*). M. Gustave and Zero (Tony Revolori) tobogganing downhill at breakneck speed in pursuit of Jopling (Willem Dafoe, *The Grand Budapest Hotel*). Royal (Gene Hackman), Ari (Grant Rosenmeyer) and Uzi (Jonah Meyerson) leaping into a swimming pool, showjumping in the park as Buckley dashes past in the foreground, and riding go-karts around an underpass (*The Royal Tenenbaums*) – a shot that directly references the car chase in William Friedkin's 1971 film *The French Connection*, which also stars Gene Hackman. Or a young space cadet suspended in mid-air by a jet pack in *Asteroid City*.

Lartigue once said, 'I have never taken a picture for any other reason than that at that moment it made me happy to do so.' He viewed the world through a curious, childlike lens: one of his earliest photographs, taken when he was just nine,

shows his collection of toy cars arranged in front of a cabinet in his bedroom; even at this young age, he somehow knew to place the camera on the floor to give the scene a child's-eye perspective, and to position the cars against the cabinet to convey a sense of scale. A 2009 BBC documentary about Lartigue's life and career was appropriately subtitled *The Boy Who Never Grew Up*. Given the playful, nostalgic tenor of his films, Anderson could be described the same way.

Anderson has also embraced the hyperkinetic spirit of Lartigue's work to more mature thematic ends. Although not primarily known for making violent films, Anderson is adept at shooting action sequences that often result in disaster, whether the tone is comedic, as in the shootout with the pirates in *The Life Aquatic with Steve Zissou* (one of whom is seen wearing a Texas Longhorns hat, the team of Anderson's alma mater, the University of Texas), or tragic, as in the drowning scene in *The Darjeeling Limited*. Moreover, if Anderson and Lartigue were to meet in another life, they would no doubt bond over their shared fascination with depicting vehicular crashes. In addition to Atari's (Koyu Rankin) plane in *Isle of Dogs* (2018) and Eli's (Owen Wilson) vintage Austin-Healey in *The Royal Tenenbaums*, *Castello Cavalcanti* (2013) features a hapless racing driver (played by Jason Schwartzman) who wrecks his motor in the middle of a quaint Italian village.

LEFT: *Zissou in his Tire-boat* (1911) by Lartigue.

OPPOSITE: Anderson's 2013 short film *Castello Cavalcanti* features a statue of Jesus Christ (top) which is identical to the one seen at the start of Fellini's 1960 film *La Dolce Vita* (bottom).

FROM ROME WITH LOVE

Castello Cavalcanti may have been produced for Prada, but it was born out of Anderson's love for another Italian icon. The eight-minute short was made at Cinecittà Studios in Rome, where Federico Fellini shot parts of *La Dolce Vita* (1960), *8½* (1963), *Amarcord* (1973) and other features throughout his fabled career. In 2013, a plaque containing a quote from Fellini was unveiled outside his favourite soundstage at Cinecittà:

> When I'm asked what city I'd like to live in, London, Paris or Rome, to be honest my answer is Cinecittà. Cinecittà Studio 5 is actually my ideal place; this is how I feel before an empty stage, a place to be filled and a world to be created.

Anderson has his own history with Cinecittà: most of the interior scenes for *The Life Aquatic with Steve Zissou* were filmed there, including the large-scale model of the *Belafonte*. In *Castello Cavalcanti*, the statue of Christ into which American Formula 1 driver Jed Cavalcanti crashes is the same one that flies over Rome in *La Dolce Vita*. After dusting himself off and settling his nerves with a shot of the local liquor, Schwartzman's character discovers that the village's residents might be distant relatives of his. Perhaps this was Anderson's way of acknowledging not his ancestral but his spiritual connection to Italy and its most celebrated filmmaker.

'JUST CLOSE YOUR EYES AND HOLD YOUR BREATH AND EVERYTHING WILL TURN REAL PRETTY.' – ROY NEARY

directed by

Wes ANDERSON

OPPOSITE: Rock scene:
Parts of *Close Encounters
of the Third Kind* were
filmed on location at the
Devils Tower National
Monument in Wyoming
(top); imposing rock
formations are similarly a
key feature of Anderson's
own alien invasion movie
Asteroid City (bottom).

PART 4
Close Encounters of the Third Kind

(Steven Spielberg, 1977)

When Anderson was in the fourth grade, he began writing and producing one-act plays inspired by, among other things, the 1970s TV cop show *Starsky & Hutch*, which Anthony (Luke Wilson) and Dignan (Owen Wilson) can be overheard discussing in the short version of *Bottle Rocket* (1994). Amateur dramatics became a coping mechanism for Anderson, a way of shielding himself from the painful breakdown of his family. In a 1999 interview with *SFGATE*, he explained:

> My parents were getting divorced. It was kind of horrible. I couldn't accept it for the longest time. I was having a problem with self-discipline. So this teacher who knew I liked to write plays made this deal that every two weeks that went by that I didn't have this self-discipline problem, I got to put on another play.

As previously discussed, the theme of family dissolution underpins much of Anderson's work. The same is true for Steven Spielberg, whose films have repeatedly explored the emotional repercussions of his own parents' divorce, the most recent – and pointed – example being *The Fabelmans* (2022). In *Close Encounters of the Third Kind*, protagonist Roy Neary (Richard Dreyfuss) takes a giant leap into the unknown by volunteering to board an alien spacecraft, preferring to take his chances in outer space

rather than remain on Earth with his wife and kids. While on the one hand the film presents a wholesome sci-fi adventure involving humanity's first contact with a bunch of musical extraterrestrials, the subtext of Neary's story is unavoidably bleak.

If you know where to look, signs of Spielberg's influence on Anderson can be found scattered all across his work – not just in terms of how both directors depict parent–child relationships and the effects of post-separation trauma, but also in the way they approach basic compositional techniques such as blocking and staging. Yet it wasn't until *Asteroid City* that Anderson paid direct homage to *Close Encounters of the Third Kind*, most prominently via the arrival of the UFO and the subsequent cover-up attempt by the US Army. He even goes so far as to thank Spielberg in the end credits.

Prior to this, the most obvious hint appeared in *Moonrise Kingdom* in the form of Bob Balaban's narrator, who gives a guided tour of New Penzance Island and at one point reveals that he helped Sam earn his orienteering badge. Before becoming one of Anderson's regular players, Balaban was probably best known for playing cartographer-turned-translator David Laughlin in *Close Encounters of the Third Kind* (alongside one of Anderson's heroes, François Truffaut). In both films, Balaban interrupts a group of characters by exclaiming, 'Excuse me!'

Asteroid City moves between two crisscrossing narratives: the first is a black-and-white TV documentary, presented in a boxy 4:3 aspect ratio, which details the making of a fictional play with the same title as the film; the second is an imagined production of said play, shot in sun-bleached anamorphic widescreen, which revolves around a 1955 convention of Junior Stargazers and Space Cadets hosted in a remote town in the California-Nevada desert, where the only clouds in the sky are generated by a nearby nuclear test site.

These budding young geniuses are joined by their parents, chief among them being Jason Schwartzman's Augie Steenbeck, a recently widowed war photographer, and Scarlett Johansson's Midge Campbell, a discontented Hollywood star. It's worth mentioning that most of the film's adult cast, including Schwartzman and Johansson, take on multiple roles, adding an extra dimension to Anderson's tried-and-trusted frame story method. As Anderson explained to EW after the film's Cannes premiere, 'The story we're telling is a play, and we are both telling the story of the making of the play, and also the story of the play itself. The making of the play is about people who tell stories.'

Anderson has listed Archie Mayo's *The Petrified Forest* (1936) and John Sturges' *Bad Day at Black Rock* (1955) as key inspirations for *Asteroid City*, as well as the plays of Elia Kazan, the films of John Ford, and the golden era of Looney Tunes cartoons (1944–64), as evidenced by the intermittent presence of a lifelike Road Runner type puppet. The *Looney Tunes* connection is particularly relevant in the context of *Close Encounters of the Third Kind* – when Neary experiences an epiphany that leads him to construct an enormous model of Devils Tower, the Wyoming landmark where he will eventually come face to face with the aliens, his daughter can be seen watching Marvin the Martian on TV in the background.

Speaking of model making, both *Close Encounters of the Third Kind* and *Asteroid City* feature several awe-inspiring instances of forced perspective, an in-camera effect where miniatures are filmed at a precise angle and distance to make them appear closer or farther away than they truly are. It's a form of optical illusion Spielberg and Anderson have each employed to great effect throughout their careers; the baffling discovery of a cargo ship in the middle of the Gobi

Desert in *Close Encounters of the Third Kind* and the majestic Monument Valley-like rock formations that prick the horizon in *Asteroid City* are two of the best examples.

Asteroid City contains subtle references to various elements from other Spielberg films, such as the hand-painted Fourth of July billboard from *Jaws* (1975) and the industrial-grade plastic tunnels from *E.T. the Extra-Terrestrial* (1982). But it is *Close Encounters of the Third Kind* that exerts by far the biggest gravitational pull on Anderson's film. While the central character's abandonment of his family betrays a more cynical side to Spielberg, it is telling that, before joining up with the aliens, Neary shares a tender kiss with a single mother who has been on the same transformative journey as him. In *Asteroid City*, two strangers experience a similar spiritual attraction.

Augie and Midge are wounded souls who are each missing a piece of themselves. Over the course of the film, they confide in each other and bond over their shared sense of detachment, as well as their mutual dependence on the camera. The brief yet intimate relationship they strike up ultimately brings them both closure and a renewed appreciation for life. Reflecting on his motivations for making the film, Anderson has said:

We're probably most concerned with death. These are the biggest milestones in our lives. The losses. Maybe that's what movies are about, or so I think. About the cosmic power of our lost loved ones.

THE THEME OF FAMILY DISSOLUTION UNDERPINS MUCH OF ANDERSON'S WORK; THE SAME IS TRUE FOR STEVEN SPIELBERG

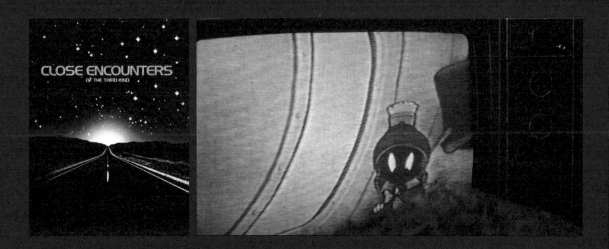

ABOVE: The ominously altered billboard in *Asteroid City* (top) is a clear reference to the graffitied 4th of July sign in *Jaws* (middle).

The official US theatrical poster for *Close Encounters of the Third Kind* (bottom left).

While *Asteroid City* contains a Road Runner-like puppet, another *Looney Tunes* star, Marvin the Martian, makes a brief appearance in Spielberg's film (bottom right).

VIEWING RECOMMENDATIONS

1. *City Streets* (Rouben Mamoulian, 1931)
2. *Grand Hotel* (Edmund Goulding, 1932)
3. *Trouble in Paradise* (Ernst Lubitsch, 1932)
4. *King Kong* (Merian C. Cooper, Ernest B. Schoedsack, 1933)
5. *L'Atalante* (Jean Vigo, 1934)
6. *Toni* (Jean Renoir, 1935)
7. *Little Lord Fauntleroy* (John Cromwell, 1936)
8. *Nothing Sacred* (William A. Wellman, 1937)
9. *Bringing Up Baby* (Howard Hawks, 1938)
10. *You Can't Take It with You* (Frank Capra, 1938)
11. *The Women* (George Cukor, 1939)
12. *The Mortal Storm* (Frank Borzage, 1940)
13. *Sullivan's Travels* (Preston Sturges, 1941)
14. *The Talk of the Town* (George Stevens, 1942)
15. *The Life and Death of Colonel Blimp* (Michael Powell, Emeric Pressburger, 1943)
16. *La Belle et la Bête* (Beauty and the Beast, Jean Cocteau, René Clément, 1946)
17. *My Darling Clementine* (John Ford, 1946)
18. *The Lady from Shanghai* (Orson Welles, 1947)
19. *Drunken Angel* (Akira Kurosawa, 1948)
20. *The Fallen Idol* (Carol Reed, 1948)
21. *Letter from an Unknown Woman* (Max Ophüls, 1948)
22. *The Queen of Spades* (Thorold Dickinson, 1949)
23. *Man on a Tightrope* (Elia Kazan, 1953)
24. *Summer with Monika* (Ingmar Bergman, 1953)
25. *L'oro di Napoli* (The Gold of Naples, Vittorio De Sica, 1954)
26. *Bad Day at Black Rock* (John Sturges, 1955)
27. *Les Diaboliques* (The Devils, Henri-Georges Clouzot, 1955)
28. *Rififi* (Jules Dassin, 1955)
29. *The Man Who Knew Too Much* (Alfred Hitchcock, 1956)
30. *Sweet Smell of Success* (Alexander Mackendrick, 1957)
31. *Mon Oncle* (My Uncle, Jacques Tati, 1958)
32. *Good Morning* (Yasujirō Ozu, 1959)
33. *The World of Apu* (Satyajit Ray, 1959)
34. *The Apartment* (Billy Wilder, 1960)
35. *L'Avventura* (The Adventure, Michelangelo Antonioni, 1960)
36. *Classe tous risques* (The Big Risk, Claude Sautet, 1960)
37. *Zazie dans le Métro* (Zazie in the Metro, Louis Malle, 1960)
38. *Lola* (Jacques Demy, 1961)
39. *The Exterminating Angel* (Luis Buñuel, 1962)
40. *The Insect Woman* (Shôhei Imamura, 1963)
41. *Jason and the Argonauts* (Don Chaffey, 1963)
42. *The Pink Panther* (Blake Edwards, 1963)
43. *Station Six-Sahara* (Seth Holt, 1963)
44. *A Hard Day's Night* (Richard Lester, 1964)
45. *Les parapluies de Cherbourg* (The Umbrellas of Cherbourg, Jacques Demy, 1964)
46. *Rudolph the Red-Nosed Reindeer* (Larry Roemer, 1964)
47. *The World of Henry Orient* (George Roy Hill, 1964)
48. *Alphaville* (Jean-Luc Godard, 1965)
49. *Le bonheur* (Happiness, Agnès Varda, 1965)
50. *Blow-Up* (Michelangelo Antonioni, 1966)
51. *The Taking of Power by Louis XIV* (Roberto Rossellini, 1966)
52. *Who's Afraid of Virginia Woolf?* (Mike Nichols, 1966)
53. *Mouchette* (Robert Bresson, 1967)
54. *Titicut Follies* (Frederick Wiseman, 1967)
55. *The Conformist* (Bernardo Bertolucci, 1970)
56. *The Out-of-Towners* (Arthur Hiller, 1970)
57. *Santa Claus is Comin' to Town* (Jules Bass, Arthur Rankin, Jr, 1970)
58. *A Clockwork Orange* (Stanley Kubrick, 1971)
59. *The King of Marvin Gardens* (Bob Rafelson, 1972)
60. *Amarcord* (Federico Fellini, 1973)
61. *American Graffiti* (George Lucas, 1973)
62. *La grande bouffe* (The Big Feast, Marco Ferreri, 1973)
63. *Wrong Move* (Wim Wenders, 1975)
64. *The Bad News Bears* (Michael Ritchie, 1976)
65. *Next Stop, Greenwich Village* (Paul Mazursky, 1976)
66. *L'Homme qui aimait les femmes* (The Man Who Loved Women, François Truffaut, 1977)
67. *Days of Heaven* (Terrence Malick, 1978)
68. *Girlfriends* (Claudia Weill, 1978)
69. *Black Jack* (Ken Loach, 1979)
70. *Winter Kills* (William Richert, 1979)
71. *One from the Heart* (Francis Ford Coppola, 1981)
72. *They All Laughed* (Peter Bogdanovich, 1981)
73. *The French* (William Klein, 1982)
74. *The King of Comedy* (Martin Scorsese, 1982)
75. *Missing* (Costa-Gavras, 1982)
76. *Shoot the Moon* (Alan Parker, 1982)
77. *À nos amours* (To Our Loves, Maurice Pialat, 1983)
78. *The Right Stuff* (Philip Kaufman, 1983)
79. *Love Streams* (John Cassavetes, 1984)
80. *The Razor's Edge* (John Byrum, 1984)
81. *Mishima: A Life in Four Chapters* (Paul Schrader, 1985)
82. *Prizzi's Honor* (John Huston, 1985)
83. *Witness* (Peter Weir, 1985)
84. *Something Wild* (Jonathan Demme, 1986)
85. *Barfly* (Barbet Schroeder, 1987)
86. *Moonstruck* (Norman Jewison, 1987)
87. *Akira* (Katsuhiro Ôtomo, 1988)
88. *School Daze* (Spike Lee, 1988)
89. *Drugstore Cowboy* (Gus Van Sant, 1989)
90. *The Plot Against Harry* (Michael Roemer, 1989)
91. *Sex, Lies, and Videotape* (Steven Soderbergh, 1989)
92. *An Angel at My Table* (Jane Campion, 1990)
93. *Slacker* (Richard Linklater, 1990)
94. *To Sleep with Anger* (Charles Burnett, 1990)
95. *Only Yesterday* (Isao Takahata, 1991)
96. *Olivier, Olivier* (Agnieszka Holland, 1992)
97. *Porco Rosso* (Hayao Miyazaki, 1992)
98. *It All Starts Today* (Bertrand Tavernier, 1999)
99. *Gosford Park* (Robert Altman, 2001)
100. *Rois et reine* (Kings and Queen, Arnaud Desplechin, 2004)

WES ANDERSON FILMOGRAPHY

FEATURE FILMS

Bottle Rocket (1996)
A trio of slackers go on a short-lived crime spree
across Texas in a bid to become master thieves.

Rushmore (1998)
An eccentric teenager competes with a tycoon for a
teacher's affection at a prestigious Houston prep school.

The Royal Tenenbaums (2001)
A highly dysfunctional upper-middle-class family are
reunited in this comedy of manners set in New York City.

The Life Aquatic with Steve Zissou (2004)
An unethical oceanographer risks his life and reputation
in order to avenge his best friend in this nautical caper.

The Darjeeling Limited (2007)
Three estranged brothers rekindle their sibling rivalry
while embarking on a spiritual train journey across India.

Fantastic Mr. Fox (2009)
A proud and cunning fox finds himself in a high-stakes
game of chicken with some particularly irritable farmers.

Moonrise Kingdom (2012)
Two precocious young misfits set off an island-wide search
after running away together in 1960s New England.

The Grand Budapest Hotel (2014)
A concierge and his protégé pursue a priceless painting
in a fictitious wartorn Eastern European country.

Isle of Dogs (2018)
A boy travels to a dystopian wasteland on the outskirts
of a futuristic Japanese city to retrieve his lost dog.

The French Dispatch (2021)
An anthology of stories concerning the residents of
a fictional French city over the course of several decades.

Asteroid City (2023)
A theatrical troupe rehearses a play about a space convention
interrupted by an alien in an American desert town.

SHORT FILMS

Bottle Rocket (1994)
Hotel Chevalier (2007)
Prada: Candy (2013)
Castello Cavalcanti (2013)
Come Together: A Fashion Picture in Motion (2016)
The Wonderful Story of Henry Sugar (2023)
Poison (2023)
The Ratcatcher (2023)
The Swan (2023)

MUSIC VIDEOS

Tip-Top: 'Aline' (2021)

COMMERCIALS

American Express: *My Life. My Card.* (2006)
SoftBank (2008)
Stella Artois: *Le Apartomatic* (2010)

INDEX

IMAGE CREDITS

Cover and interior illustrations by Lorena Spurio.

The publisher wishes to thank all of the film production and distribution companies, and publishing companies, whose images appear in this book. Special thanks also to the following for images. We apologize in advance for any omissions, or neglect, and will be pleased to make any corrections in future editions.

7 Entertainment Pictures/Alamy; 12 PictureLux/The Hollywood Archive/Alamy; 15 l Fred W. McDarrah/MUUS Collection via Getty Images; 15 r © Columbia Pictures/Courtesy Everett Collection/Alamy; 19 t World History Archive/Alamy; 19 bl AP Photo/Harry Harris/Alamy; 20 t Pictorial Press Ltd/Alamy; 22 t Trinity Mirror/Mirrorpix/Alamy; 24 b Vinyls/Alamy; 25 t JACQUES MARIE/AFP via Getty Images; 26 Thao Nguyen/Fox Searchlight/PictureGroup/Sipa USA/Alamy; 27 Trinity Mirror/Mirrorpix/Alamy; 30 Everett Collection, Inc./Alamy; 36 l BFA/Alamy; 37 b From www.fforfilms.net (essays on the movies by Joshua Wilson); 43 t United Archives GmbH/Alamy; 44 t Everett Collection Inc/Alamy; 46 l OgreBot; 46 r Everett Collection, Inc./Alamy; 47 t Everett Collection Inc/Alamy; 48 l Searchlight Pictures, painting by Michael Taylor; 48 r The Picture Art Collection/Alamy; 49 t Album/Alamy; 52 CPA Media Pte Ltd/Alamy; 53 tr DAIEI FILMS/Album/Alamy; 53 br Photo 12/Alamy; 58 t Gino Circiello owner of 'Gino of Capri' restaurant featuring 'Zebras Wallpaper', 1986. Image courtesy of Scalamandré. www.scalamandre.com/zebras; 59 tr Frank Tozier/Alamy; 60 t PictureLux/The Hollywood Archive/Alamy; 60 b Entertainment Pictures/Alamy; 61 l Album/Alamy; 61 r CBW/Alamy; 64 Photo 12/Alamy; 65 br Don Smith/Radio Times/Getty Images; 67 l Everett Collection Inc/Alamy; 70 l SHOCHIKU FILMS/Album/Alamy; 70 r Photo 12/Alamy; 72 l Associated Press/Alamy; 72 r Everett Collection Inc/Alamy; 76 l Everett Collection, Inc./Alamy; 76 r Photo 12/Alamy; 82 Album/Alamy; 83 t Everett Collection Inc/Alamy; 86 Everett Collection, Inc./Alamy; 88 tr Richard Schubert (CC BY-SA 3.0 DEED); 88 br Zoonar GmbH/Alamy; 89 bl Library of Congress Prints and Photographs Division; 89 br Library of Congress Prints and Photographs Division; 93 bl Album/Alamy; 93 br Renn Productions/Photo 12/Alamy; 96 b API/Gamma-Rapho via Getty Images; 97 bl Ismoon (public domain); 97 br © The Pasternak Trust; 99 tl Robert Elfstrom/Villon Films/Gety Images; 99 bl Granger/Bridgeman Images; 103 Michelangelo Oprandi/Alamy; 104 Everett Collection, Inc./Alamy; 105 bl Bettmann/Getty Images; 105 r Norman Rockwell, © The Brown & Bigelow Licensing Company; 110 r Everett Collection Inc/Alamy; 111 br Everett Collection Inc/Alamy; 112 t Everett/Shutterstock; 114 l Records/Alamy; 116 t © Touchstone/courtesy Everett Collection/Alamy; 116 b Everett Collection Inc/Alamy; 117 tl Stanislav Traykov (CC BY-SA 3.0 DEED); 117 tr AP Photo/Jean-Jacques Levy; 120 l Paramount Pictures/Cinematic/Alamy; 121 t Everett Collection Inc/Alamy; 121 bl Bob Chamberlin/Los Angeles Times via Getty Images; 121 bc Paramount Pictures/Album/Alamy; 126 © 50th Street Films/Courtesy Everett Collection/Alamy; 127 bl Photo © Minneapolis Institute of Art/Gift of Paul Schweitzer/Bridgeman Images; 127 r Newscom/Alamy; 128 t Metropolitan Museum of Art, New York; 129 tl Photo © Edward Burtynsky, courtesy Flowers Gallery, London; 133 t United Artists/Woodfall/Album/Alamy; 133 br Trinity Mirror/Mirrorpix/Alamy; 134 t Jeff Gilbert/Alamy; 136 tr Photo © Bonhams; 136 bl kim sayer/Alamy; 136 br arkerphotography/Alamy; 137 t DcoetzeeBot (public domain); 139 t 20th Century Fox/ Album/Alamy; 139 bl A7A Collection/Photo 12/Alamy; 139 br Greg Williams/© Fox Searchlight Pictures/Everett Collection/Bridgeman Images; 142 t Everett Collection Inc/Alamy; 142 b Simon Tranter Photography/Alamy; 143 bl Retro AdArchives/Alamy; 143 bc © Avco Embassy/courtesy Everett Collection/Alamy; 143 br © United Artists/courtesy Everett Collection/Alamy; 149 t MeijiShowa/Alamy; 152 Films A2/Ciné Tamaris/Album/Alamy; 156 l World History Archive/Alamy; 156 r d' Ora/ullstein bild via Getty Images; 157 Geoffrey Taunton/Alamy; 160 Everett Collection, Inc./Alamy; 164 PjrStatues/Alamy; 167 t Peter Barritt/Alamy; 167 bl Culture Club/Getty Images; 167 br Three Lions/Hulton Archive/Getty Images; 170 r ScreenProd/Photononstop/Alamy; 173 l Trzęsacz (public domain); 176 l Warner Bros/Photo 12/Alamy; 176 r Warner Bros/Allstar Picture Library Limited./Alamy; 180 RANK/Album/Alamy; 181 br Allstar Picture Library Ltd/Alamy; 184 t Lewenstein (public domain); 186 Dcoetzee (public domain); 187 t BotMultichillT (CC BY-SA 4.0 DEED); 188 BFA/Twentieth Century Fox/Alamy; 189 Digital image, The Museum of Modern Art, New York/Scala, Florence; 190 tl © 1998 Kate Rothko Prizel & Christopher Rothko ARS, NY and DACS, London. Photo: Private Collection. Photograph Courtesy of Sotheby's, Inc. © 2023; 190 tr © 1998 Kate Rothko Prizel & Christopher Rothko ARS, NY and DACS, London. Photo: Gift of The Mark Rothko Foundation, Inc., National Gallery of Art, Washington 1986.43.173; 193 tr © 1998 Kate Rothko Prizel & Christopher Rothko ARS, NY and DACS, London. Photo © Christie's Images/Bridgeman Images; 193 b © 1998 Kate Rothko Prizel & Christopher Rothko ARS, NY and DACS, London. Photo: akg-images; 194 t Photograph by Jacques Henri Lartigue. © Ministère de la Culture (France), MPP-AAJHL; 196 Photograph by Jacques Henri Lartigue. © Ministère de la Culture (France), MPP-AAJHL; 197 b LANDMARK MEDIA/Alamy; 201 bl Allstar Picture Library Ltd/Alamy; 208 © Liz Seabrook.

BIOGRAPHIES

About the Author

Adam Woodward is a writer and semi-lapsed critic. He is the Editor-At-Large at *Little White Lies* magazine, and has been watching films for a living since 2009. He lives in London with his partner Liz, who took this photograph.

About the Illustrator

Lorena Spurio is an italian illustrator based in Rome. Born in Reggio Calabria, she has also lived in Madrid, Barcelona, Turin and Milan. She studied literature and art history but then fell madly in love with illustration. Proud alumni of Mimaster Illustrazione 2022 (Milan).

AUTHOR ACKNOWLEDGEMENTS

The Worlds of Wes Anderson is the first book is the first book I have written for Frances Lincoln/Quarto, and I am grateful to everyone there who has had a hand in its making. First and foremost, to commissioning editor John Parton, who approached me with a rough outline of the project in the spring of 2022 off the back of a somewhat ill-fated (through no fault of either of ours, I hasten to add) Wes-themed book we had worked on together a few years earlier. Thanks for showing faith in me, for your astute guidance – and for the flat whites.

I am equally indebted to my editor, Laura Bulbeck, who did so much behind-the-scenes to bring this book to life. Your thoughtful suggestions and unerring support have been invaluable. A hearty shout-out to senior designer Isabel Eeles for overseeing the art direction, and huge thanks to lead designer Claire Warner for the gorgeous page layouts and typesetting; your meticulous attention to detail is worthy of Wes himself. Thanks also to Sarah Chatwin, Ann Barrett and Eliza Walsh for all your efforts proofreading, indexing and on production, respectively. And massive thanks to illustrator Lorena Spurio for producing such a stunning cover, not to mention the charming spot illustrations that adorn each chapter. I feel incredibly lucky to have my work bolstered by your collective talents.

For providing constructive, insightful feedback on my manuscript and steering me in the right direction on several topics, thanks to Michael Leader; I cannot overstate how much your sharp-eyedness and all-round enthusiasm for this book helped me. My eternal gratitude also extends to fellow Wes-head Sophie Monks Kaufman, who is not only the most gifted writer I know but damn good company to boot; I invariably came away from our semi-regular (usually cocktail-oriented) catch-ups feeling re-energized and with my thinking sharpened.

Thanks to my dear family for showing a keen interest in this book from the outset (despite Wes not really being their cup of darjeeling), and to my cherished friends and colleagues for giving me encouragement and allowing me to witter on about all things Wes, especially David Jenkins, Hannah Strong, Tertia Nash and Elena Lazic. Writing something of this size and scope is never straightforward, but it's a whole lot easier when you're surrounded by the best people. On that note, the final and deepest thanks must go to my partner Liz – my Rushmore – for being my guiding star not just on this project but in life generally. This book is dedicated to you.